STORIES
GRANDPARENTS
Tell About
Their
GRANDCHILDREN

Bill Adler

GRANDPARENTS
Tell About
Their
GRANDCHILDREN

WHEELER
PUBLISHING, INC.
ROCKLAND, MA

★ AN AMERICAN COMPANY ★

Published in Large Print by arrangement with Quill, an imprint of HarperCollins Publishers, Inc., in the United States and Canada

Wheeler Large Print Book Series.

Set in 16 pt Plantin.

Library of Congress Cataloging-in-Publication Data

Adler, Bill, 1929-
    Stories grandparents tell about their grandchildren / Bill Adler.
        p. (large print) cm.(Wheeler large print book series)
    ISBN 1-58724-219-2 (softcover)
    1. Grandparent and child. 2. Grandparents. 3. Grandchildren.
4. Large type books. I. Title. II. Series.

[HQ759.9 .A36   2002]
306.874'.5—dc21   2002022313
                                                                        CIP

With love to our granddaughters—
Karen, Madeleine,
Claire, and Amanda

Many thanks to John Malone for his
creative work
in connection with this book

contents

introduction

Many children have been heard to say that Grandma or Grandad understands them better than Mom and Dad. That can be true in some ways, simply because most grandparents have arrived at a point in their lives where they are largely at peace with themselves and their views of life. They have a clear vision that goes back a long way, and they have settled many issues in their minds and hearts that may still be troubling their grown children. Having raised those children, they have gained a perspective that allows them to see their grandchildren in the light of wisdom gained. Looking back, they can see where they might have done things a little differently, been more sympathetic with a child at one point or a little firmer at another. With their grandchildren, they have a chance to put that knowledge to fresh use, to make the most of all that they have come to understand about children through the years.

The relationships between grandparents and grandchildren often have a special richness that enhances the lives of both. Grandchildren learn much from their grandparents, and bask in the warmth of their love. Grandparents derive great satisfaction from watching a new generation of family members explore the world and seek out their own unique place in that world. Grandparents tell their grandchildren stories, all kinds of stories, made-up ones and true ones, funny ones

and instructive ones, that help those youngsters to find their way. And the grandchildren
provide the grandparents with new stories to
tell. The antics and achievements of grandchildren make for very good stories indeed.

This is a book of such stories, told by
grandparents about their grandchildren.
They are the kind of stories told to other
grandparents, shared both with old friends
and new acquaintances. In our very mobile
society, even grandparents are constantly
meeting new people, and they get to know one
another by telling stories about their grandchildren. Stories about grandchildren are
terrific ice-breakers, sometimes better for
that purpose than stories about oneself.
Retired grandparents who have moved to
the Sunbelt, say, use such stories to get
acquainted with new neighbors—they serve
as an invitation to friendship. At the same time,
of course, the teller of the story is able to
deepen the bond he or she feels with the
much-loved grandchild. The telling of the story
can almost make it seem as though the child
is there.

You will find all kinds of stories in this book.
The grandparents who tell them come from
all walks of life and many different parts of
the country. Their stories about their grand-
chilchen may be amusing or poignant; they may
be little stories that strike a familiar chord
or dramatic stories filled with suspense. But
they are always suffused with pride, and,
now and again, a bit of boasting—that is a
grandparent's privilege. There are stories

about the pranks and confusions that are part of the life of every small child, and stories about the courage and achievements of older grandchildren. There are tales of the adventures shared by grandparents and their grandchildren, some filled with the almost magical enchantment of the perfect day spent in one another's company, and others about genuine dangers met and overcome. Some grandparents tell of how they helped a grandchild solve a knotty problem. Others movingly recount how a grandchild did something wonderful for them.

These are stories about real life, and the difficulties and challenges of the world, as well as its wonders and its joys, are reflected here. But there are no unhappy endings. Grandparents know all about persevering and overcoming, and the stories they like to tell one another must have an ending that satisfies. The stories grandparents tell each other about their grandchildren are, above all, affirmations of life.

1

how cute they are

Babies and toddlers can be adorable, but it is when children begin to talk that things start getting really interesting. As youngsters begin to explore the world and try out new words to describe it, their attempts to understand the innumerable mysteries that surround them can be endearing, surprising, and often very funny. They can also be embarrassing. The parents of young children can sometimes find their kids more exasperating than amusing, but the same out-of-place question or remark that may cause a parent to wince is often greeted with delight by a grandparent. Partially this is because grandparents usually spend less time with a child than parents do, and thus are less likely to feel their patience unraveling. But it is also true that a grandparent may be happy to rediscover the pleasures that young children provide. Having seen their own children through the traumas of adolescence and concerns of young adulthood, it can be a tonic to encounter once again, in a different context, the half-forgotten antics of childhood, now newly minted by another generation.

The grandparents you will meet in this first chapter fondly recount how their young grandchildren made them laugh with the kind of telling question kids are so good at asking, astonished them with a surprisingly acute grasp of reality, or touched them with an act of childish bravado. A small hand held out under the porch light, a com-

1

ment that shouldn't have been made, a word mispronounced, a concept misunderstood, or a plot being hatched to get something a child wants may be small events, but ones that bring joy to the doting grandparent. Whether it's a boy trying to catch Santa Claus in the act or a mock wedding for nine-year-olds, such moments find their special place in the memory book of every grandparent.

"How cute they are," we murmur.

The Telltale Hand

Many grandparents I know don't get to see their grandchildren nearly as much as they'd like to. People in this country are always on the move, and it can mean a flight clear across the country to visit a son or daughter. That often means that your grandchildren are almost like different people every time you see them. But my wife Helen and I were lucky—or half lucky. We live in Cleveland, and our daughter is all the way out in Seattle, but our son Mike is only a block and a half away.

I've been a movie theater owner all my adult life. When Mike went away to college I had two theaters in Cleveland, as well as various other real estate interests. After college, to my surprise and certainly to Mike's surprise, he decided to go into business with me. This was in the Seventies when the multiplexes were really getting going. That's what attracted Mike—the chance to do something new.

So I was able to watch his kids grow up:

Steven, who's in his last year of college now, and Diana, who's a freshman. Of course, we celebrated all the major holidays together, but some of my favorite memories involve Halloween. Since Helen and I were right around the corner in Shaker Heights, Steve and Diana always came trick-or-treating, and it was a treat for us to see the lengths they'd go to to disguise themselves so we wouldn't recognize them. My daughter-in-law Susan is very gifted at sewing—she does all the costumes for our community theater—so she was always able to fulfill the kids' fantasies when it came to costumes. Of course, the very fact that Steve and Diana had the best costumes of anybody who came to our door gave them away every time, although we didn't let them know that.

When Steve was nine, he came dressed as an alien. He looked like something from the bar scene in *Star Wars*, with tentacles on his head and great bulging eyes. Diana was dressed as a ladybug. They were cute as all get-out. About an hour later, when we thought we'd seen the last of the troops for that Halloween, the doorbell rang again. When I opened the door, there was a single child, with a simple costume, just a sheet over his head and a cowboy hat. There weren't even any eyeholes in the sheet, and since it was after dark, I kind of wondered how he was getting around the neighborhood, but I guessed he must be raising the sheet between houses and then putting it back down again just before he rang the bell.

The cowboy ghost didn't say anything, just held out his hand. As I was putting some candy in it, I suddenly recognized whose hand it was. Steve was making a second appearance for the night. His hands had deeper lines in the palm than most kids his age, and he had very squared-off fingers—I'd have known that hand anywhere. I didn't let on, of course. He closed his hand over the candy and said thank you in a high squeaky voice, and turned and dashed down the steps. I took a peek out the front window and saw him stop and lift the sheet at the bottom of the front walk. When I told Helen who our visitor had been, she wanted to call up Mike and Susan and tell them not to worry if they discovered their son was missing. But I persuaded her not to. I had a hunch he'd try the same game with his parents and I didn't want to spoil the fun.

The next day at the office, I asked Mike if he'd had a late visit from a lone cowboy, and he laughed and said, "Hit you, too, did he?" Mike had recognized Steve's hand just as I did.

Helen and I and Steve's parents kept our mouths shut about having seen through Steve's game for years. We finally told him about it on his fifteenth birthday. He shook his head and said, "Boy, you can't get away with anything, can you?" But he was very impressed we'd stayed quiet about it for so long. He told us he'd gone home with his sister after the regular round, and then decided to see if he could fool his parents and us. He pulled the sheet right off his bed, but he didn't dare cut holes in it to see through. The cowboy hat wasn't his. A friend had forgotten it a couple of days before. Steve confessed that he couldn't see a thing. "I'm surprised I didn't fall down your front steps, Grandpa," he said.

I should add that Steve's going to the UCLA film school after he graduates from college. He says he thinks our theaters could use some better movies.

—*Stan, 63*

A Cat in Heaven

Every couple of weekends, my husband and I have a long-distance telephone conversation with our grandchildren: Art, who's ten, and Amy, who's seven. We often find ourselves laughing after one of these conversations, because Art and Amy say very amusing things sometimes. When talking with other grandparents, we've often wondered why it is that things that made us impatient when our own children were young seem so delightful in grandchildren. I suppose it's simply the fact that it's not a day-in, day-out relationship.

Still, every now and then Mort and I find ourselves at a loss for words. Not long ago, for instance, when Amy got on the line, she announced, "My cat is dead."

Now, losing a pet is serious business at any age. So, I very sympathetically said, "Oh, I'm so sorry, Amy. That's very sad."

Mort, who was on the extension, asked,

"How did it happen, Amy?" Mort is one of those people who believes in facing things squarely, so of course he would try to elicit the grisly details. And in this case it was grisly.

"He was run over by a dump truck," Amy said.

"Did you see it happen?" Mort asked.

"Mort . . ." I said.

"No," Amy replied. "I found him all squashed when I came home from school."

"You must have been very upset," I said.

"Of course," said Amy, in that tone that suggests you're awfully dumb. "I cried for a long time."

"Are you going to get a new cat?" Mort asked.

"If Daddy will let me," said Amy.

Now, our son is a dog person, and Art has a dog. I had a feeling that our boy John would suggest a dog for Amy, too. He was never mean to cats, but he always thought they were only interested in themselves and didn't really care about human beings.

"Did your father say no?" asked Mort.

"I haven't asked him yet," said Amy. "I liked the one I had. I miss him."

"Well," I said, "at least he's in heaven."

Amy came right back, saying, "Daddy didn't even like my cat when he was alive. Why would God want a cat that's squashed dead?"

That stopped me cold. Besides, I could just hear Mort saying to me, "You know, Iris, a cat heaven also suggests the existence of a cat hell." So I just couldn't think of a word to say. I hoped Mort might take up the slack, but he was as speechless as I was.

Fortunately, Amy had something else to say. "I think I'm going to ask for a parrot instead. I wanted one, but Daddy said a cat and a parrot wouldn't be a good idea. So now I guess I can have a parrot."

Mort finally found his voice again. "That's a good idea, Amy. Parrots can't get run over since they stay in the house in a cage."

"No," said Amy, "I want one I can carry around on my shoulder. I saw a man doing that on television."

"Was he a pirate?" Mort asked.

"Don't be silly," said Amy. "He was an animal trainer."

"Would you like to be an animal trainer?" I asked.

"Maybe." There was a slight pause. "Do you think I could train a parrot to answer for me when Mom calls from downstairs?"

Mort chuckled. "I think you could. But I wouldn't tell your parents about that idea if you want to get a parrot."

"Hmm," Amy said. "Thanks, Grandad. You're smart."

That's par for the course in my family. I try to say soothing things about cat heaven, and Mort upstages me by telling Amy how to outwit her parents. I'll tell you one thing. When that parrot bites the dust I'm not saying one word about heaven.

—*Iris, 57*

𝓛ast summer, while my son-in-law was on National Guard duty, my daughter came to visit me and her father for two weeks. We were delighted, because it was our first chance to spend extended time with our grandson Tommy. He was just two years old, walking around on his own, and beginning to talk. My husband has always been wonderful with kids. He's a great storyteller, whether he's making the story up or reading aloud and acting it out. We still had a lot of our children's storybooks around the house, and my husband had little Tommy in gales of laughter reading him tales, about Goldilocks and the three bears, and the three little pigs and the big bad wolf.

But the three little pigs story had unfortunate consequences. We have a dear friend, a widower named Sam, who is a very large man. He came over to visit one weekend afternoon, and of course my daughter, who knew Sam well herself, brought Tommy out to meet him. Tommy was a little shy at first, and hung back a bit, but then he settled down on the floor while the rest of us talked. There was a brief pause in the conversation, and Tommy raised his arm—and pointed at Sam and said, extremely clearly, "Pig, pig."

My daughter said, "Tommy!" I rolled my eyes and said, "Sorry, Sam." My husband just clapped a hand to his forehead.

But Sam was wonderful. He smiled at Tommy and said, "I'll bet your grandfather's been reading you the story about the three little pigs, hasn't he?"

My husband spread his hands, pleading guilty.

"Well," Sam said. "That's a wonderful story. And it's all about me."

Tommy stared at him wide-eyed.

"That's right. I'm all grown up now, but I was the third little pig, the one who was smart enough to build a house out of bricks so the wolf couldn't get me."

My husband laughed and said, "And he's been building them ever since. Sam's built half the new houses in town."

Tommy said, "Huff, huff."

Sam smiled even more and said, "You can huff and puff all you want, Tommy, but you won't be able to blow one of my houses down."

By then we were all laughing, and Tommy began to giggle away, and what could have been a social catastrophe turned into a cherished moment. As I say, Sam was always a dear friend, but that afternoon gave us an even greater appreciation of him. Sam always did know how to turn a debit into a credit.

—*Louise, 62*

A Theological Question

My son Michael, his wife, Beth, and my delightful grandson Todd came to spend Christmas with us last year. They live in

North Carolina and my husband and I live in northern Pennsylvania. It was the first time Todd had seen snow, and he was just thrilled. We dragged Michael's old sled down from the attic and Todd had a wonderful time zooming down the hill back of the house. The entire visit was a delight, but my favorite moment came on Christmas Eve, when we went to the carol service at our church. Todd was just five, and I think he was beginning to understand the religious meaning of Christmas a little. We sang all the famous carols at the service, "Oh, Come All Ye Faithful," and "Hark the Herald Angels Sing," and "Silent Night." Todd has a very strong little voice and he sang out with great conviction. But in the car on the way home, he suddenly asked me a question. "Granny," he said, "I don't understand about 'Silent Night.' Why is yon Virgin round?"

Todd was sitting between Beth and me in the back seat, and we kind of looked at each other, and we just couldn't help it, we burst out laughing. Todd was quite offended, of course. I tried to explain that the Virgin wasn't round, actually, but the song was talking about light around her and the baby Jesus. He seemed to accept that, but my husband, who can be quite naughty, said, "Why is the Virgin round? Now there's a theological question for the ages." And of course we all started laughing again. Poor Todd was very perplexed, and quite annoyed. No wonder kids want to grow up so fast. They're just trying to get the jokes.

—Anne, 56

Where's Charley?

$\mathcal{W}$e are lucky enough to spend every Christmas with our daughter Susan, her husband, Hank, and our three grandsons. Some grandparents are not that fortunate. Alan and I know at least three couples our age who've never spent Christmas with their grandchildren. Oh, they get telephone calls, but that's hardly the same thing, is it? Mind you, those couples tend to boss people around a bit, and that may have something to do with why they're not invited. We try very hard not to get in Susan and Hank's way, or spoil their daily routine. When we talk on the phone at Thanksgiving, Hank always says, "Now, don't forget, we're all panting to see you on Christmas Eve!" A nicer young man you couldn't ask for.

So Alan and I pack up the car and make the five-hour trip. One year there was supposed to be a bad snowstorm, so we left a day early and spent the night at a motel about an hour away from Susan and Hank's. We didn't want to put them to any trouble by arriving a day early, but we were afraid they might call and get worried about us if they didn't know what was happening. So we just told them we were going to take our time and stop off somewhere along the way.

Every year, as soon as we get in the car, Alan says, "Got the camera?" And I point to it hanging around my neck. This is a running joke, because one year I did forget it, and we had to buy a new one before we got there. Alan can't be without his camera. We must have a thousand pictures of our grandsons. They're all put into albums—I do that part—and though I'm sure they'd bore anyone else to death, we love looking at them. It's such fun to see how the boys have grown from year to year.

When we drive up to Hank and Susan's house, all heck breaks loose. The kids come running out to the car, and we all hug and jump around and say "Merry Christmas" until we're exhausted. It's wonderful. The front of the house is all trimmed with lights, and when we go inside, the tree almost makes me want to cry, it's so beautiful. Susan is a real artist about making things look pretty. Takes after me, of course. And that's a terrible lie.

My favorite story about Christmas with our grandchildren happened two years ago. We managed to get them all packed off to bed about ten o'clock, after Hank read "'Twas the Night Before Christmas" aloud. When Santa Claus arrives in the story, Alan starts doing all these gestures and putting his finger alongside his nose, that kind of thing. He does have something of a bowlful of jelly aroud the middle these days, poor dear. Anyway, the kids love it, and just howl with laughter. And then we put all the presents under the tree and went up to bed ourselves. Alan and I slept like logs, of course, after the trip.

About seven in the morning that Christmas, we heard noises downstairs, and managed to get ourselves wide enough awake to stagger downstairs. Susan and Hank were in the kitchen making blueberry muffins. That's a tradition in their house. Billy and Michael were sitting on the floor in the living room staring at the presents and waiting for the green light to start tearing Santa's goodies open. Billy was seven that year, and Michael was nine. But there was no sign of little Charley, who was three. I asked Susan where he was, and she said, "Oh, Charley's in a hiding stage. He'll turn up." Well, I went upstairs and started looking in closets and under beds, but there was no sign of him. I was getting a little worried by the time I came down again. His brothers had been very quiet, just as they're supposed to be. They're allowed to sit by the tree, but they can't touch anything and they have to be quiet. But I asked them if they knew where Charley was. They shook their heads, and I wondered aloud if he'd gone outside. I guess my worry showed, because Billy and Michael started shouting, "Charley, Charley!"

There's a table in the living room with an antique shawl over it, and suddenly Charley crawled out from underneath it. He'd obviously just woken up and he had sleep in his eyes, but he kind of shook himself and said, "Did I miss him? Did I miss him?" Then he dissolved in tears. The poor kid had snuck downstairs after the rest of us fell asleep, and was hiding out under the table trying to catch Santa in the act. But of course, he'd fallen asleep, too. The child was stiff as could be after lying on the floor all night.

Hank told Charley you couldn't catch Santa, no matter how hard you tried, but if Charley was going to insist on trying, would he please leave a note next year telling us where he was sleeping on Christmas Eve.

Charley recovered from his disappointment very quickly, and of course at three you're just beginning to really enjoy Christmas, so he had the time of his life. But I'll never forget him crawling out from under that table, looking like a tiny little Rip Van Winkle. "Did I miss him?" What a treat.

—*Irene, 64*

Vocabulary

My granddaughter Katie loves big words. She'll pick up on one she's heard on television, or from her parents' conversation, and it will pop up unexpectedly a day or two later. Of course, she doesn't always get the meaning quite right, or she'll substitute a word that sounds similar for the correct one. I'm a high school English teacher, and I hear some very odd things in my own classroom. Not just mispronunciations, like "athalete" for "athlete"—which is hard to combat since so many professional sports heros and even sports reporters get it wrong. I'm talking more about the boy who said a girl had a "radium" smile. He meant "radiant." I told him he better stay away from that girl because she was too hot to handle. About half the class got it. Things like that can be a trifle discouraging when you're dealing with seventeen-year-olds. But Katie's only six, and I find it very amusing when she does it. And, of course, she *is* my granddaughter.

Last month, Katie was a flower girl at my niece's wedding. My daughter Elaine, Katie's mother, was matron of honor. It was a big church wedding, with a splashy reception afterward. They threw rice at the bride and groom when they left the church, and then confetti when they left the reception. We were standing on the steps watching the bride and groom drive away, and I looked down at Katie and asked her if she'd had a good time being a flower girl. She was pushing at her hair with her hand, and she said, "Yes, Grandma, but I wish they wouldn't throw all that confederation. How am I going to get all this confederation out of my hair?"

I didn't even try to correct her. I was just trying to keep from laughing. How indeed do you get confederation out of your hair? Whole countries have been stumped by that one!
—*Marilyn, 59*

The "Wedding"

We've all seen a hundred movies where the seven-year-old boy says, "I hate girls." But it isn't always true, and I can prove it. This is about my grandson Arnie and the new girl on the block, whose name was Alice-Anne.

Until he was seven, Arnie paid no attention to girls at all. He and some other boys in the neighborhood had a gang called the Demons of Dayton. They held their secret meetings in a tree house. I knew it well, because it was in my backyard, and my father had built it for me in 1936. My son Ted made it his headquarters, too. I had to make some repairs before the Demons could take it over, but it was good to see the old place getting some use.

My wife and I live just two blocks from Ted and his wife Marilyn, and Arnie was over visiting all the time. One day at the end of the summer when Arnie was seven, we were playing catch on the side lawn when we saw a moving truck pull up to the house across the street. The new family that was moving in arrived at the same time. We stopped to watch, nosy like all neighbors when new people move in, and we saw Alice-Anne Tucker for the first time. She was just Arnie's age, and pretty as they come. She had dark red hair, but no freckles. Arnie had bright red hair and lots of freckles. I swear I heard a thunderclap when the eyes of those two kids first met, across the street from each other. Arnie waved and Alice-Anne waved right back and that was the beginning of it. The next day, when my wife took over a chocolate cake as a welcoming present, Arnie announced that he was going too, and the formal introductions were made.

From then on Arnie and Alice-Anne were inseparable. Arnie asked her to join the gang, over the protests of the other boys in the Demons of Dayton. But since Arnie held the lease, so to speak, on the tree house, they had to give way. Soon enough, though, the boys kind of drifted away.

By November, things had gotten to the point where Arnie asked his parents at dinner if Alice-Anne could sleep over the following Saturday night. My daughter-in-law said that she hadn't realized the Tuckers were going away, but if Alice-Anne needed a place to stay, the guest room was always available to her. Arnie replied that the Tuckers weren't going away and he thought Alice-Anne could use the lower bunk in his room. My son Ted choked on his meatloaf and my daughter-in-law dropped her fork on the floor. Needless to say, that sleep-over didn't happen.

Nevertheless, Arnie and Alice-Anne decided they wanted to have a wedding the following summer. They were almost nine then, and, according to them, they'd been engaged for six months. So both sets of parents got together and talked the whole thing over and decided that a mock wedding could be kind of fun for everyone. It was explained, very thoroughly, to both Arnie and Alice-Anne that this was just a pretend wedding, play-acting, you know. Now, some people seem to get the wrong idea about all this. It was just a game. Ever hear of having fun? Anyway, we had the ceremony in Alice-Anne's backyard in August. The "bride" wore white shorts and a pink halter top. The "groom" wore cut-off jeans and a T-shirt. I played the minister. And I emphasize "played" here. The only things I have a license for are driving and duck-hunting. The ceremony was made-up, and was based heavily on Professor Irwin Corey, if you remember him from the old days on Johnny Carson. We all had a great time, and consumed great quantities of lemonade and grape juice. More civilized than a lot of weddings I've been to, thanks to the lack of booze.

Well, of course you know how it is with kids who get married too young. I hate to tell you this, but they were divorced at eleven. Didn't speak to each other for nearly two years. They became friendly enough again in high school, but they never dated. They went off to different colleges, and then they met again in New York when they were starting out in their first jobs. That thunderclap boomed again, and this past summer, at age twenty-three, they got married again. This time the bride wore a white gown with an eight-foot train, and the groom was twice the height he'd been the first time around. Everyone drank champagne, but I slipped them a bottle of grape juice, wrapped up to look like a million dollars, which I insisted they had to open when they reached the hotel in the Bahamas where they spent their honeymoon. The card said, "In memory of old times." They sent me a card that said, "Thanks for the memory, Reverend Grandpa." I thought that was kind of nice.

—*Arnold, 71*

2

going adventuring

"How dost thou like adventuring?"
Don Quixote asks Sancho Panza in
Man of La Mancha.
    The love of going adventuring is one
of the most cherished bonds shared by grandparents
and grandchildren. Because parents are invari-
ably very busy, grandparents are often given the
privilege of introducing a grandchild to some of
the special wonders that the world has to offer. Going
adventuring may involve making an excursion
to a sporting event, a concert, or the theater. It may
mean packing up and taking a trip. But adven-
turing can also take place right at home, as a
grandparent reads a book aloud or teaches a
grandchild how to do something. Sometimes,
when the child is older, it may even be that the
child teaches the grandparent—an especially
rewarding adventure on both sides.
    As you will discover in this chapter, the adven-
ture can be as simple as a fishing lesson—but of
course the catch must have something special
about it. An outing to the ballpark is always an
adventure, and once in a while it can turn into
a day when great things happen, providing mem-
ories to be cherished and retold for a lifetime. A
journey to another place, with grandparent and
grandchild exploring together, can bring not only
new sights and activities, but a shared hilarity that
becomes memorable in itself. Going adventuring
can also bring unexpected risk, and the sense of

19

triumph that comes from meeting and overcoming adversity.

But the best thing about going adventuring is that both child and grandparent usually get to discover new things about themselves as well as the world around them, enriching and deepening the relationship between them.

The Fishing Lesson

A year ago I woke up with a lot of pain in my chest. I was scared, I admit it. My wife Gracie called an ambulance, and off we went to the hospital. Turned out that it wasn't as bad as it felt—just an everyday, run-of-the-mill heart attack. No triple bypass or anything like that needed to keep me going. But during that short ride, I did see chunks of my life pass before my eyes. Almost like flashbacks. I saw people I haven't thought about in thirty years. Miss Douglass, my second-grade teacher, was there, screaming at all us kids. She was a mess, should have been locked up, and we were terrified of her. I thought, please don't let me meet my maker with Miss Douglass's face in my mind. But the show went on. Gracie and me on our wedding day, our daughter Polly on *her* wedding day. And then there were my grandsons, Clay, Clive, and Clint. Believe me, Gracie and I had nothing to do with naming them—not that we object. But we don't want to take—shall we say—credit for the three C's.

The funny thing is that the images of the boys that went through my head all had to do with fishing. I taught them all to fish. My favorite story about that was teaching Clint. He was about six at the time. I took him out on his own, so his older brothers wouldn't be laughing at him when he made mistakes. Older brothers have a way of doing that.

I baited the hook for Clint, who was a little squeamish about all those worms squirming around in the can. We were sitting there on the pier in the sun with our lines in the water, and after about five minutes there was a big pull on his fishing rod. That kid got so excited! He practically yelled, "Grandpa, I got one." And a minute later, he was saying, "Grandpa, I think I need some help. It's gotta weigh forty pounds!" I had to laugh—how many times had I said that!

So I gave him a hand. It did feel like a forty-pounder, but I knew it wasn't a fish. So after a good fight we reeled it in. As I thought, it was a turtle. Probably only about twenty pounds, but they feel heavier on a line because they're so solid, and they can't whip around in the water the way a fish does. Clint said, "Oh, boy, it's a turtle. I've caught a pet turtle. What'll we name him?"

I had planned to throw him back, but Clint was so thrilled with his catch. "I'll be the only one with a pet turtle, Grandpa. What should we call him?" I was removing the hook very carefully, so I wouldn't do any more damage, and the turtle wasn't making it easy. "How about Fighter," I said. "Oh, great,"

Clint replied happily. But I knew we were going to have our own fight on our hands when we got home. My daughter wasn't going to be too happy about this addition to the household, I was pretty sure.

And sure enough, Polly took one look and said, "No. No, no, and no." Well, Clint started crying, and his brothers jumped in on his side. Clay pointed out that there were two rock pools in the backyard for Polly's goldfish. My daughter was trapped and she knew it. "How long do these things live?" she asked. "Well," I said, "it depends on the kind, but some of them live longer than humans." "Wonderful," Polly said. "I suppose I'll have to add a codicil to my will, to see he gets taken care of after I'm gone. Clint, of course, will have gone off to live in some city apartment, and Hank and I will be stuck with the damn critter for the rest of our lives." Polly has this way of exaggerating problems a little. But she knows it, and she was beginning to smile. "What's his name, anyway? I assume you two have already named him?"

"*Her* name," I said very quickly, "is Polly Jr."

My daughter put her face in her hands and groaned, but we all started laughing and she joined right in.

"His name is Fighter," Clint said.

"It's funny," Polly said, "but when I woke up this morning and the birds were singing and the lake was glistening out there, I thought, something wonderful is going to happen today. This isn't what I had in mind, but I guess it'll have to do."

That was ten years ago. The boys put in a third pool in the backyard for Fighter, and he's still going strong. Lying in the ambulance, flashing back to the day we caught him, I thought, "I'll be damned if that turtle's going to outlive me." That's when I began thinking I'd be okay. So me and Fighter, we're still going to hang around for a while.

—*Freddie, 71*

Theater Is Not the Movies

When I was growing up in the 1940s, my parents took me to the theater as often as possible. They weren't wealthy, but when a special treat was in order, it often meant going to the theater. My mother had grown up in Montclair, New Jersey, and she started going to Broadway shows when she was very young. She actually saw *Peter Pan* with its first star, the famous Maude Adams. Another time, she went to the ballet and actually saw Nijinsky in *The Spectre of the Rose*, where he entered leaping through a window and seemed to cover half the stage before he landed. My father grew up in Missouri and didn't get to New York until he was in his late twenties, but then he would go to the Ziegfeld Follies and saw all the greats, Fanny Brice, whom Barbra Streisand later played in *Funny Girl*, and Will Rogers twirling his ropes and making jokes.

When I was a child, I saw the D'Oyly Carte company from England perform almost all the

Gilbert and Sullivan operettas when they came to the United States on tour. I saw Yul Brynner in the original production of *The King and I*, and Ray Bolger in *Where's Charley?*, and Jean Arthur and Boris Karloff in a wonderful revival of *Peter Pan*. When I became a mother, I saw to it that my own daughter and son got to the theater a lot, too—of course, that had nothing to do with my own pleasure! Actually, children are a wonderful excuse to indulge yourself in new productions of your own favorites. I loved introducing my children to shows I had first seen when I was much younger. To keep the generational link alive, I took them to see Sandy Duncan in *Peter Pan*, and my daughter took her two girls to see the Cathy Rigby production.

More recently, I took my older granddaughter, Jenny, to see the Broadway musical *Titanic*, which had won the Tony Award for Best Musical before the movie with Leonardo DiCaprio came out. By the time we went to the Broadway show, Jenny, who's eleven, had already seen the movie twice. I was a little worried that she would be expecting the same story. Of course, I'd seen at least one movie a week when I was growing up too, and I knew that I'd always enjoyed seeing a Broadway version of something, even if I'd already seen a movie based on the same story. But even though Jenny had been to a lot of theater, I wanted to make sure she understood that this was very different from the movie.

We were standing in the lobby of the theater before going in to take our seats, and I was saying once again how different she'd find it. I somehow had the feeling she hadn't quite grasped what I'd been saying. Suddenly, something seemed to dawn on her, and she looked straight up at me and said, "You mean, Leonardo's not in it?" Her eyes were absolutely wide with shock. I had to laugh. I said no, he wasn't, but I thought she'd like it anyway. "Well," she said, in a tone that meant, "We'll see about that."

Fortunately, she did like the Broadway show very much. And afterward she said something very wise. "You know, Grandma, when you know there aren't any special effects, and it's happening right in front of you, it's almost more spectacular, isn't it?" So I think we have another generation of committed theater lovers in our family.

—*Jane, 65*

A Wild, Wild Day

My-ten-year old grandson, Melvin, got very depressed the last weekend of September in the fall of 1999. That was the weekend that his beloved New York Mets went down to Atlanta to play the Braves and lost all three games. The Mets were just three games behind the Braves that Friday, and if they won all three, they'd be tied for first place, with a chance to win their division title—never mind get the wild card berth that seemed more likely. But by the end of that dismal weekend, they were suddenly six games back, and in trouble even for a wild card spot. When I stopped by my son's house in Astoria late Monday afternoon, Mel opened the door and said, very glumly, "Hello, Grandpa," in a way that suggested his dog had just died. I felt so sorry for him. And I knew just how he felt. I'd grown up in Boston as a Red Sox fan, and being a Red Sox fan is a truly excruciating form of masochism—a tale of woe everybody knows. When I moved my family to New York in the 1960s, I kept my allegiance to the Red Sox— I certainly wasn't going to become a fan of their main rivals, the Yankees. But I also began to root for the Mets, and got my reward when they won the World Series in 1969. But then, of course, I had to suffer through the 1986 Series between the Red Sox and the Mets, when the Red Sox were one pitch away from winning the Series, and then managed to lose not just that game, but the seventh game and the whole Series to boot.

My son Ted—he was named for Ted Williams of the Red Sox—became a Mets fan too, and passed that on to Mel. The Mets were a pretty lousy team through most of the 90s, when Mel was a little kid, but they improved a lot in '98, and last year they were a true contender for the last half of the season. Mel was really excited, and it was awful watching them go down the tubes that weekend in Atlanta. I'd watched the Saturday game with Mel and my son, and I really felt for my grandson. He kept sinking lower and lower into the couch, as though he wanted to disappear.

I'd bought tickets for the three of us to go to the last game of the season the following Sunday, October 3, at Shea Stadium. I figured that the Mets would at least have the wild card berth sewed up by then, and maybe, just maybe, they might be tied with the Braves, and that game could decide the championship. Either way, it seemed like a good game to see. But as that final week wore on, and the Mets lost to the Phillies, who were twenty games behind them, and then blew another one to the Braves at Shea, it looked as though they were out of it altogether. My idea of getting tickets for the final game began to seem like a really bad one.

But then the Mets beat Pittsburgh at Shea on both Friday and Saturday, and Houston and Cincinnati were still fighting it out in the Central division. There was a chance, a small one, but at least a chance, that the Mets could still get into the playoffs if they won that last game. They might have to get through an extra game on Monday to make it, but they'd still be alive. So as we took our seats along the third base line, my grandson was upbeat again, and we went over all the possibilities of how things might turn out. I was praying the Mets would win the game, not just because their season deserved a playoff spot, but for Mel's sake.

It was a beautiful afternoon for baseball, the kind of "fall classic" day that makes you feel really alive. Mel sat between me and Ted and kept swinging his head back and forth between us, chattering like a little monkey. The whole crowd was excited, but things got pretty silent for a bit when Pittsburgh scored a run in the first inning. I thought maybe we were in for a long, disappointing afternoon, but of course I told Mel that there was a long way to go yet. It's amazing the optimism a ten-year-old can inspire in a grandfather.

Then the Mets pitcher, Orel Hershiser, who'd had a really bad day on Tuesday, getting lifted after making only one out, settled down. When the Mets got a run in the fourth to tie Pittsburgh, I thought Mel might pass out from excitement. Neither team got a run in the fifth, or the sixth, or the seventh, or the eighth. That makes for an exciting game anytime during the season, but on the last day, with everything on the line, it makes for a tension that can be almost unbearable. I was glad I'd taken an extra half-dose of my blood pressure medication that morning. It was discovered that I had high blood pressure right after the Mets/Red Sox Series of '86, so I blame baseball for the whole thing.

So there we were in the ninth inning. Pittsburgh had one runner on, and Armando Benitez came in to pitch for the Mets. He gave up an intentional base-on-balls to set up a double play, and Mel grabbed my hand on one side and his father's on the other. Lo and behold, the Mets were safely out of the top half of the inning and had a chance to win the game in the bottom of the ninth. As any fan knows, baseball is not just a game of Hall of Fame stars, but also of unlikely heroes. We were about to get one of the latter. His name was Melvin

Mora, who'd had only four hits for the Mets the whole season, but who'd been brought in as a pinch runner in the seventh and played left field. Yes, that's right, his first name is Melvin. Don't think we didn't make a lot out of that when he smashed a one-out single to right field. "Hey," I said to my grandson, "You Melvins are quite something, aren't you?" And Ted began chanting, "Melvin, Melvin," at the top of his lungs until my grandson punched him in the arm.

Mora managed to get to third base, diving in head-first even though there was no throw, when Edgardo Alfonso hit another single to right. We were all on our feet screaming, with my grandson pumping his arms in the air like crazy. As I said, we were sitting on the third base side, so we had a great view of what happened next. Pittsburgh brought on a guy named Brad Clontz to pitch, and he intentionally loaded the bases. Then Clontz had to pitch to the Mets' biggest star, the catcher Mike Piazza. We looked down at Melvin Mora, and he was watching Clontz like a hawk. We didn't know it until later, but Mora and Clontz had been teammates in the minors, so Mora knew how Clontz pitched. He was waiting for a mistake Clontz had made before. And it happened. Clontz threw a wild pitch to Piazza. It bounced in the dirt and headed for the backboard. Mora took off like a jackrabbit, and jumped on home plate with both feet. Well, the stadium went nuts. Down on the field the Mets were going nuts. As has happened so many times before, a little-known player

29

had come off the bench and made himself into a hero. The game was won, the season saved— the Mets would win their one-game playoff for the wild card berth 5–1 the next night in Cincinnati—and the hero's name was Melvin. As we were heading out of the stadium, my grandson Mel looked up at me and said, "Gee, Grandpa, you sure do know how to get tickets to the right game!"

—*Doug, 62*

With the Rope in His Teeth

I spend a lot of time with my grandson Jason. My daughter Maggie and Jason's father are divorced. It's a friendly divorce as things go, and so many of Jason's friends are in that same situation that he doesn't seem to find it strange at all. How things have changed, says the windy old guy. But they have. When I was fourteen, Jason's age, I felt sorry for friends whose parents were divorced, because there were so few of them. Of course, it was my own generation that made divorce really popular, but my wife Ruth and I are still together after thirty-six years. Some people think we're a little smug about that, I guess, and I suppose we are. It's not that we didn't have problems, but we managed to get through them and we're proud of it. I'm not going to apologize for that.

At any rate, Jason lives with his mother, who works. He sees his dad and his stepmother regularly, and he gets along fine with everyone. But the divorce has meant that for the last six years, Jason has come up from New York to spend July and August with me and his grandmother in Ipswich, Massachusetts. Maggie always comes up for a couple of weeks on her vacation, and Jason usually goes off to spend a couple of weekends with his father, but for the most part he's with Ruth and me for the summer months. As far as we're concerned, that's a great treat.

Most people don't know much of anything about Ipswich. If people outside of Massachusetts have heard of it, it's usually because the writer John Updike lives here. Ipswich is a small town, so of course we know him to say hello to, but that's about it. I have a law practice here, pretty low-key for the most part, which is just fine by me. It leaves me with plenty of time to go sailing in the summer. Don't start imagining any fifty-foot yacht; that's not the kind of sailing I mean. I'm talking about small sailboat racing, boats with a mainsail and a jib, and not really meant for more than two people.

Maggie and I used to race every weekend in summer when she was a kid, and now I do it with Jason. I taught him to sail and he's very good. We win a fair number of races. I think I'm going to buy him his own boat next summer so we can can race against each other. I know how that will end up. Jason more than proved that he's ready for his own boat at the end of last summer.

The harbor at Ipswich is quite sheltered, protected from the open Atlantic by a long narrow island. The harbor is big enough to race in, and we don't venture out into open waters too often. It's a very safe place to sail, and there's been a yacht club here for a century or more. People from twenty or thirty miles inland keep their boats here, and things get pretty lively in summer. The racing is very competitive, and there are lots of kids involved.

But the real racing mecca in Massachusetts is Marblehead, down the coast. They hold a race week every year, and boats from the entire coast travel there to take part. Some boats are hauled out of the water and taken down on boat trailers behind cars and vans. But the contingent from Ipswich always gets there by using a tow. A big Chris Craft or other powered yacht can tow a dozen small sailboats behind it, connected by a heavy rope tow line that passes back from boat to boat. The boats being towed have their sails down, of course. The rope is attached at the bow and stern of each boat, and runs down the middle of it. The boats are like beads on a necklace, strung out behind the tow boat. The sailboats do keep their rudders attached, so the owners can help to steer and keep the tow straight in the water.

Last summer, the tow was scheduled on a Saturday. As it happened, there was a considerable storm Friday night. I was a little concerned about having a tow go out in the aftermath of a nor'easter, but younger and more adventurous—or foolhardy—heads prevailed, and we set off at eleven in the morning. The minute we got out of Ipswich Harbor, I knew we'd made a mistake. The water was very rough, with nine-foot swells. Swells aren't real waves, they're rolling undulations, and they don't have white caps on top, so they don't really look dangerous. But that's deceptive, and they were a particular problem for a tow line. Because there were valleys of water between each swell, the dozen boats on the tow line weren't like stones on a necklace but like knots in a whip, and that whip was getting cracked every two minutes. The Chris Craft itself wasn't having any trouble cutting through the water, but the whole tow line was snapping like crazy, and the farther back you got, the worse it was.

Our boat was about halfway back on the tow, where the whip really started to crack. Suddenly, the rope that joined us to the boat behind us snapped. We were still attached to the tow, but the six sailboats behind us were now adrift. This happened just off Crane's beach, which is the best beach along that whole stretch of coast, with beautiful white sand. We went there almost daily for a swim. But at that moment it looked pretty ominous. The problem was that the boats behind us were adrift only about three hundred yards off the beach, and because the water gets shallow very quickly there, the Chris Craft wouldn't be able to circle around more than once to pick them up and get them re-attached. If it couldn't be managed, the loose boats would be washed up on the beach, where the breakers were really crashing in on the shore. Not only might you have a lot of badly damaged boats, but it was the kind of situation in which someone could easily get cracked on the head and drown when the boats tipped over in the breakers.

Jason had been kind of excited about the swell when we first got out of the harbor. "Wow," he'd said, "this is going to be like an amusement park ride." But he'd quickly realized that the tow line was having an awful lot of stress placed on it. He'd also been the first to notice that the people in the boat behind us were in trouble, even before the tow line snapped. Their rudder had jumped out of its sockets, and they hadn't been able to get it back in. The tow people in the boat were a mother and son. She was in her late thirties and her son was about nine. They were fairly new to sailing, but they'd learned fast. They'd even beaten us in a couple of races. The mother, Helen, did a smart and brave thing when the rudder jumped out. She was holding the tow rope itself, down the middle of the boat, against her side to keep the boat from careening around uncontrollably. I kind of winced when I saw her doing that, though—I knew she'd be black and blue for weeks.

But when the tow rope did snap, I got very concerned about their situation. Helen's son, Jerry, was a good sailor, and I knew he wasn't going to panic or anything, but he was a small kid, and I worried about how either of them was going to deal with re-attaching the tow rope when the Chris Craft circled around. Since they were the lead boat of the six that were adrift, they were going to have to be responsible for getting the whole lot of them safely tied up again.

Jason saw the problem, too. "I wish we were the lead boat of the ones adrift, Grandad," he said. "We'd be able to handle it better."

I just nodded. I was proud of him for saying that.

The rope had snapped very close to their boat. That meant that we had a long length of it that we'd pulled into our boat. They were receding behind us fast as the Chris Craft began to turn in the rough water, very slowly to avoid capsizing any of the remaining boats on the tow. When we came around, it was going to be necessary for us to throw the rope very accurately to that lead boat, and for either Helen or her son to catch it and tie it to the cleat at the bow. I asked Jason, "So, who's going to throw the rope to them, you or me?"

Jason said, "Whatever you say, Grandad."

"Well, I think you," I said. "At this point in our lives, you have the stronger arm."

"I don't know," he said. "But I'll do my best."

The Chris Craft was turning again, coming in behind the last of the drifting boats and then moving inside them, between the boats and the beach. It was clearer than ever that it wouldn't be possible to make a second pass before the water got too shallow for the Chris Craft. We had to pick up the rest of the tow now or it wouldn't happen.

The nine-year-old, Jerry, was at the front of his sailboat, ready to catch the rope. His mother had apparently decided that it was wiser for her to stay hunched down in the boat at dead center, trying to keep it stable, while her son moved up to the bow. It seemed the right move to me.

As we moved parallel to their boat, the Chris Craft cut its motors to idle. But of course the swells were still keeping both our boat and Helen and Jerry's boat bobbing pretty wildly. It was going to be very tricky. As we came athwart, but separated by about ten feet, Jason threw the line to Jerry. He caught it, leaning out over the bow. But just at that moment, his boat was swept suddenly upward with a new swell, and the rope slipped out of his hands.

I'll never forget what happened then. Jason pulled the loose rope rapidly up out of the water, placed it between his teeth, and dove into the ocean. Now, Jason is a terrific swimmer, I knew that. But my heart stood absolutely still for a moment. I turned to look at the Chris Craft ahead of us. The captain saw what was happening and put up his hand to indicate they weren't going anywhere. I looked back at Jason to see him clinging to the bow of the other boat, tying the rope to the cleat. Then he let go and Jerry looped the rope around the cleat again for good measure. Jason was back in the water, swimming as fast as he could toward our boat. I braced myself against the stern and reached down to help pull him out.

Jerry's voice came across the water—there were twenty feet between us by then and the rope was beginning to pull taut—saying that things were okay. I turned and signaled the

Chris Craft, and we heard its motor rev up really fast. The whole tow line was one again, and we began to move forward.

It was just in time. Stan, the captain of the Chris Craft, told me afterward that we had literally seconds to spare before the Chris Craft ran aground. We proceeded very slowly after that, and put in at the next port, a very small one at a place called Magnolia. They were very glad to see us, and told us that the Coast Guard had been out in helicopters looking for us. They'd missed us because they'd thought we'd be further down the coast by then, which we would have been if the tow line hadn't snapped.

All in all, it was some adventure. The kind you like to think back on, because it turned out all right, but that you'd rather not go through again. Jason was treated like a hero, of course, but he was very modest about it. He'd just shrug and say it had seemed like the most sensible thing to do. Sure, my sensible grandson, swimming through nine-foot swells with a tow line in his teeth, while Grandad looks on with his heart in his mouth.

I wouldn't have missed it for the world.

—*Glen, 57*

Skyline Drive

*F*our years ago, my daughter-in-law Moira was very ill with cancer. She'd had a mastectomy and was undergoing chemotherapy as well. It was a very difficult time for her, my son Michael, and their two boys, Larry and Peter. Moira is a lovely woman, with a wonderful sense of humor and real Southern charm—not the fake kind that covers up deep-down selfishness. Moira and I were always laughing about some of the women in town. We called them "sweetie-pies." They just dripped sugar, but the minute your back was turned, the knives came out. I know it's not usual for a woman to say this about her daughter-in-law, but I've always adored Moira. I tell Michael she's far too good for him. That doesn't bother him—he completely agrees.

Moira was very brave about being ill, and she tried very hard to behave as normally as possible. But I thought it would do her good to have at least a few days when she wouldn't feel she had to work so hard at being cheerful, and since it was summer, I suggested that my grandsons and I take a little trip together. They'd never been to Washington, D.C., even though it's just a day's drive from Lynchburg, Virginia, where we all live. But there was one small problem—I don't drive. Oh, I have a license, but I hate driving. It just scares me. I don't mind being a passenger in a car in the least, but it makes my heart pound to get behind the wheel. It makes life a little difficult since I'm a widow, but I manage.

My grandson Larry had turned sixteen five months earlier, and had his license. He was a very good driver from the start, and after a little hesitation, Michael decided that it would be all right for Larry to do the driving on the

trip to Washington. He even let us use his new
Buick. He trusted Larry that much. So we set
out at the end of June, me, eleven-year-old
Peter, and Larry behind the wheel.

Going up, we cut across to Richmond and
took I-95 up to Washington. Larry was quite
a serious boy, even at sixteen, but Peter has
always been a cut-up. And when the two of them
are alone together with me, the hidden devil
in Larry can come out, too. They tease me
dreadfully. They're always trying to shock
me by saying cynical things about the world.
I play along and tell them they're perfectly
awful. We have a very good time. On the way
up, we were talking about all the things we were
going to do in Washington. Peter asked if we
had to pay to get into the Capitol, and I said
I didn't think so. It belonged to the people of
the country, after all. Larry said, "But you do
have to bribe your congressman." Peter immediately asked, "How much?" And Larry said,
"Oh, I hear ours will settle for pennies. If you
come from New York City, it costs a lot more."
Peter said, "Well, then, I guess it's a good thing
we live in the middle of nowhere." I told
them they were just terrible.

We stopped for lunch near Richmond. Well,
not exactly stopped. Larry and Peter have
this running argument about whether to go
to McDonald's or Burger King. Larry much
prefers the hamburgers at Burger King, but
Peter is mad about the french fries at
McDonald's. I suggested that maybe there
would be a Kentucky Fried Chicken along the
way. Well, we were driving along one of those

stretches of highway where there is every fast food restaurant known to man, so Larry drove into a McDonald's where we got french fries and drinks, and then we got burgers at Burger King, and then we made a third drive-through detour to get me some fried chicken. And there we all were, driving along and munching on our favorites. Talk about a movable feast!

In Washington, we stayed at a hotel over behind the White House, but we were hardly there except to sleep. We did everything: the Capitol, the White House, the Smithsonian, the National Gallery, the Lincoln Memorial, and the Washington Monument. At the White House, Peter asked me where he could find a portrait of Eleanor Roosevelt. I asked him why he wanted to see her portrait in particular, and he said he wanted to see if it would talk to him the way it did to Mrs. Clinton. That business about Hillary "talking" to Mrs. Roosevelt was all over the TV about then. Larry said Mrs. Roosevelt didn't talk to Hillary, that was just Jay Leno exaggerating. "But," he said, "President Nixon did talk to the portraits on the walls." And he stopped dead in his tracks in front of a portrait of somebody, maybe it was Andrew Jackson, and shook his fist and said, "I am not a crook." I nearly died. Some of the people on the tour looked very annoyed, but others grinned, which made me feel a little better. Larry is a history buff, and he knows a lot, but sometimes it isn't put to what I would call "elevated use."

We stayed in Washington five days. I'd brought what I thought were sensible shoes, but on the second day I bought a pair of sneakers. People could whisper all they wanted about me being a "little old lady in tennis shoes," but at least I wouldn't be a cripple. It seemed to me we walked about ten miles in the Smithsonian alone. Both the boys were very excited by the Air and Space Museum. My favorite place was the National Gallery, and on the fourth day we split up, so I could go back there and they could spend some more time at the Smithsonian.

I suggested that we drive back south along the Skyline Drive above the Shenandoah Valley. I'd made that trip with my husband and Michael, when he was a teenager, more than thirty years ago, and I remembered it as being spectacular. Of course, I wasn't driving, and I'd forgotten how twisty the Skyline Drive was. Larry seemed to be doing fine, but at one point I said, "Oh, Larry, just look at that view." And he replied, "Grandmother, if I look at the view, we're going to be in it, looking back up." Peter thought that was very funny and I turned around to give him a look. We both kept our mouths pretty much shut from then on. Finally, we came down out of the mountains and got back on the highway, and Larry said, "Well, that was exciting. Next time we take a trip, why don't we cross Afghanistan on bicycles."

Peter really laughed at that one. He was still chuckling ten minutes later. I apologized to Larry, and said I'd forgotten what a difficult drive it was. Larry said, "I wouldn't have missed it for the world, Grandmother. Now

I figure I can handle anything." And he gave me a big grin.

When we got home, Moira was looking much more rested, and had some color back in her face. The boys kept her laughing for days with their tales of Washington. The trip really was a tonic for all of us. Moira continued to improve and eventually recovered completely. Every now and then she says how wonderful of me it was to take the boys to Washington that summer. And my reply is always the same: "My dear, I've never had more fun in my life."

—*Edith, 71*

3

what an achievement!

Grandparents love to boast about their grandchildren's achievements. It begins, of course, with the celebration of a child's first words or first steps. Although the circumstances under which those first steps are taken may differ, and the words spoken may vary from child to child, and of course language to language, such stories are essentially the same the world over. But as the children get older, their successes take many different forms, reflecting the uniqueness of every human being. As time goes on, any grandparent will find that while the small successes of a given day, month, or year fade somewhat, there will be one or two stories about a grandchild that take on special significance, and those are the ones that get repeated again and again down the years. They are the stories that are recounted to new acquaintances, and that remain well worth retelling to family and friends. They become not just stories, but hallmarks of the unique individual the child gradually becomes.

In this chapter, grandparents tell the stories of a grandson who is quite possibly destined to become a future chef, and of another who is unlikely to become a professional athlete but whose efforts to overcome his limitations may mean all the more for that very reason. You will meet a boy whose courage and generosity are demonstrated in his making a decision not to win. A grandmother movingly recalls the blossoming of a granddaughter born sightless. And the surprising third-generation manifestation of a family talent is proudly recalled.

All parents are proud of their children's accomplishments. But the stories here, the ones grandparents tell, are reflective of the special sweetness that can be derived from watching a child who is intimately connected to you, yet not your primary responsibility, meeting the challenges of life.

The Cake

We love our three grandchildren equally. To us, that's rule number one in being a grandparent: never pick a favorite. But favoring the first-born can be tempting—you've got to watch your step. For instance, one night we were all sitting at the dining room table, looking at the albums with the kids' baby pictures. Memory lane time. As we were finishing up, little Paul, who was six, said, "Hey, wait a minute. This isn't fair. Michael's picture albums are like a telephone book. And Pat's are almost as thick. Mine looks like a little paperback. What gives here?"

Good question. Dead silence. All I could think of was to say, "Kids, would you like more dessert?" and escape to the kitchen. Being a grandparent can mean walking on eggshells sometimes. I mean, what can you say? "You were an ugly kid and we didn't want to waste any film on you"? Which couldn't be further from the truth, since Paul was as cute as could be. David, our son, muttered something about running out of film. Sure. For three years running? I adore my son, but put him in a tight spot and he's as useless as I am. Poor man, he couldn't hide in the kitchen like me.

Actually, the kitchen is a special place for me and Paul. Whenever they come over and I'm cooking, he pulls up a high stool and sits there watching my every move. And asks questions. Dozens of them. This gets on my nerves. I won't even let my husband, Joe, hover around when I'm cooking. But what can you do? Paul had got it in his head—at seven, mind you—that he was going to be a great chef someday. He's always watching the cooking shows on PBS and the Discovery Channel.

If you can't beat 'em, join 'em, I say. So I

decided to put him to work. I'm not as dumb as I look. I gave him simple things to do, like peeling potatoes or tossing the salad, at first.

But he graduated from that kind of thing very quickly. When he was eight, he said he wanted to make the cake for his mother's birthday. We sat down and looked through a lot of cookbooks. I'd suggested that he use a cake mix, but he wanted to do it from scratch, which is what I do unless I'm in a very big hurry. Cake mixes are very good these days, but I'm old fashioned, and *I* can taste the difference even if nobody else can. So I pushed him toward making a very simple orange cake with just one layer, and a plain vanilla icing.

The cookbook said, "Preparation time, 10 minutes. Cooking time, 45 minutes." Well, Paul insisted on doing it all by himself. I was under strict orders not to come into the kitchen—my own kitchen! He started at one o'clock. It wasn't until four o'clock that he came out to show me the results. He'd found the cake coloring, so the icing was bright orange. Very impressive, with swirls and everything. The cake was a bit smaller than the rectangular cake pan, and I asked him if he'd tasted some. "Sure did," he said. And he had this funny smile on his face.

We all ate the main course quite quickly that night, so we could taste Paul's cake. He brought it out and cut a piece for everyone, a bit messily, but who cared. And we all dug in. Well, it was a disaster. He'd used salt instead of sugar. I thought to myself, "I'm going to eat this if it kills me." But of course his brothers wouldn't let that happen. "Salt," they screamed. And Michael, who was thirteen, said, "You little jerk!"

I thought, "Oh, poor Paul." I could have kicked myself for not checking on him while he was making it. But he just started laughing. "I made a little mistake, the first time," he said. And he slipped out of his chair and dashed into the kitchen. Then he was back in a flash with *another* cake, which he'd hidden in a lower cupboard I don't open much. This cake was absolutely delicious. No wonder he'd been in the kitchen for three hours! He'd had to make two cakes.

When he served the second cake, he said, "Michael doesn't get any. He called me a jerk." So Michael had to eat his words if he was going to eat any cake. Paul was extremely pleased with himself, and I don't blame him. Not only had he tried again when at first he didn't succeed, but he'd managed to trap his brother, who was always teasing him, in the bargain.

So I think we really are going to have a chef in the family.

—*Helen, 62*

"It's Out of Here!"

My son-in-law Ted doesn't give a rap about sports. Don't get me wrong, he's a great guy. He's a research chemist with a major pharmaceutical company, and he's

46

done some very important work. He makes very good money, enough so that my daughter Jenny doesn't need to work, but she wants to and he's never made the slightest problem about it. It's a very solid, happy marriage, and they have two great kids, Linda, who's fifteen now, and Billy, who's not quite twelve.

But I'm very interested in sports, and it bothers me a little that Ted and I can't share that interest. I was an athletic kid, and I got drafted out of high school by the Boston Red Sox. But my second year in the farm system, I tore up my knee badly while sliding into second base, and it never did get back to normal. I joined my father's business and did very well for myself, I have no complaints. I'm not sure I was good enough to get to the majors, anyway. It's not as though I've gone through life thinking I missed out on being Wade Boggs. My son Sam was the quarterback for two years at Dartmouth, so I always have him to talk to about sports. And actually the fact that Ted isn't into sports has made me closer to my grandson Billy.

Billy is not a big kid, but he's wiry and very well coordinated. He plays Little League baseball, and things being as they are with his father, it fell to me to try to help Billy along in his playing. Billy's a terrific shortstop. He's fast, he has great hands, and his throw to first base is always right on the money. But he's always had trouble with his hitting. That's not unusual for shortstops, of course. It amazes me that the two top hitters in the American League for most of 1999 were shortstops, Garciaparra for the Red Sox and Jeter for the Yankees. That's really unusual. Major League shortstops who can hit .270 are going great, and here you have these guys hitting .340, .350. That's truly amazing.

Anyway, Billy's fielding skills were good enough so that he got to play a lot, even when his average was down around .240. But he was getting taken out a lot for pinch-hitters in the late innings, especially if his team was behind, when you need some real clout at the plate. Last summer I really worked on his hitting with him. I couldn't figure out what the problem was. His swing was fine. Oh, I tried to help him make a few small adjustments, but they didn't seem to do a whole lot of good. The problem wasn't really his seeing the ball, either. He's got 20/20 vision, and he was making contact regularly, but they'd always be these ground balls that would get stopped for an out. And other teams were making too many double plays on him.

I'm a good teacher. I've got a lot of patience, and I don't get mad and I never put Billy down. You don't help anyone that way. Well, maybe you need to blow up at some hardheads who don't listen, but Billy wasn't like that. We just weren't making much progress. It's a funny thing about sports, though. You can work and work and get nowhere, and then suddenly things click. That's true in any sport. My wife likes to watch figure-skating—even got me excited about it—and you hear the top skaters talking all the time about how hard it can be to get the hang of one of those quadruple jumps they're doing these days, and then suddenly you just have it. I was hoping that would happen with Billy if we worked on things enough.

But it was getting to be the middle of August, and it hadn't happened. I went to all the games, of course, and it would be really frustrating to see Billy lifted for a pinch hitter. But sometimes the coach would leave him in when the game was really tight and his fielding skills were too important to lose. That happened in a game in the third week of August. The teams were three-all in the eighth, so Billy got to bat. He was first up for his team in the inning, so there'd still be a chance to do something if he didn't get on base.

The count was at two balls and two strikes. The opposing pitcher had been getting stronger in the course of the game. All the runs for Billy's team had come in the first three innings, and one of those was on an error. Then Billy got a fastball a little on the outside. I saw him take a half step into it, not just leaning and swatting at it, and I thought, "That's the boy." And lo and behold, he really connected with it. You can tell by the sound, that solid *thwack* you get when a bat gets a ball just right. My eyes followed the ball up over the infield and beyond it. It wasn't too high and I thought it would probably be caught. But still, I liked the sound I'd heard, and even a line drive out to deep center would be progress for Billy. At least it wasn't on the ground.

And then I heard the man next to me—he was the father of the pitcher on Billy's team—

say, "It's out of here!" And he nudged me in the ribs with his elbow so hard I nearly fell over.

And sure enough, he was right. A home run! And not just any home run, either. It would be Billy's first in Little League ball. I swiveled my head to look back at Billy, and he was still standing at the plate, watching the ball. He had this expression on his face that said, "I don't believe this!" And then he did believe it, and this huge grin broke out on his face, and he threw the bat aside and started running the bases. And I mean, he ran. None of that home run trot stuff. He ran as though it was a sacrifice fly and he could be thrown out at home plate. Just took off like a rabbit.

The whole team was jumping up and down in the dugout, and the next batter up practically knocked Billy over giving him a bear hug after he crossed home plate. That home run turned out to be the winning margin that day. Billy didn't get taken out in the late innings after that. He didn't get any more home runs in the few remaining games, but he got a couple of solid long hits that dropped in and scored a couple of runs. I'm sure this year will be even better.

After the game, I went up to Billy and said, "Congratulations, that's the way to do it." And he looked up at me and said, "It's your coaching that did it, Grandpa. About time, I guess."

Well, of course that made me feel pretty good. But as we were driving home I couldn't help thinking that it was too bad Billy couldn't have been saying that to his dad. On the other hand, it does go to show that a grandfather can make a difference in a kid's life. And I have to say that his father got pretty excited about it all, too. He may not give a damn about sports, but he knew how important that day was to Billy and treated it accordingly. As I say, Ted's really a great guy.

—*George, 62*

The Spelling Bee

I'm what's called a "history buff." Or, as my daughter would put it, a "history nut." My wife jokes about it. She says most of her friends are either golf widows—because their husbands spend all weekend on the course—or football widows, from September though January when the NFL and college games are on television. "But," she says, "I am unique. I'm a history widow. Jim is always watching the History Channel or some program on A&E or the Discovery Channel." Actually, I don't watch as much as she makes out, because if it's a program about a subject I know well, I tend to get annoyed because things are being over-simplified. When that happens, I turn it off so I won't push my blood pressure up another notch.

This all started when I was about eleven and read *A Tale of Two Cities*. I was fascinated, and started reading all kinds of books about the French Revolution. The head librarian at our public library thought I was reading

51

books that might be too adult, and called up my parents to find out if it was all right. They hadn't gotten beyond high school, but they had a great respect for education, and they said it was fine by them for me to read anything I wanted to. So the librarian, Miss Hopkins, became my ally. She taught me the Dewey decimal system, and for four summers when I was a teenager, I worked at the library, doing everything from shelving books to adding new cards to the file drawers.

I met my wife Bea at the University of Michigan, where we both went to college. She has a mathematical mind, and teaches high school math. Put me through law school doing that, for starters. Both our kids, Adele and Jack, got her gift for math. Jack was killed in Vietnam, to our great sorrow. But Adele has three kids, Greg, Beth, and Susan. And my reading gene popped up again in Greg. He was way ahead of most kids his age in learning to read. And he was terrific at spelling. He could spell "chrysanthemum" at the age of five.

We live in Iowa, where there's a great emphasis put on education. Easterners think of Iowa as a farm state, and it is, of course, but we also send more of our high school graduates on to college than any other state in the Union. People should keep that in mind when they wonder why the Iowa caucuses are so important in presidential politics. Iowans are very big on contests—from livestock and cooking competitions at the state fair to educational ones. In our town, one of the big events of the year is the annual spelling bee. It's held at the high school auditorium at night, and every seat is taken. There have already been elimination contests at each level, and the finals can get pretty exciting. There's one at the fifth- and sixth-grade level, and another at the seventh- and eighth-grade level. We often send kids on to state and national contests; they're that good.

Greg won the local contest when he was in both the fifth and sixth grades. The boy who came in second both years was his friend Denny. Denny comes from a family that's had a very hard time. They lost their farm a few years ago, and it's been a struggle for them ever since. He has two older brothers, big strapping boys, but he's small and thin, and wears glasses. I don't think his family knows quite what to make of him. But he's very smart and I suspect he'll do just fine in life. I've acquired quite a library over the years, and Greg and Denny come over and look at books a lot. I lend them anything they want. Well, that's not quite true. They're not ready for Faulkner yet.

To get back to the spelling bee, last year Greg and Denny moved up to the top group, the seventh and eighth graders. Some of the eighth graders were very good, but there was a general feeling that Greg and Denny could beat them. Over the past several years, the prizes for the spelling bee have been getting fancier. It used to be just books, but then a couple of restaurants got into the act and added dinners or lunches for the whole family of the top three finishers. Good publicity, I suppose, but I'm sorry to see the contest commercialized that way. Then last year they had money prizes for the first time. A man who won the contest about 25 years ago set up a fund to award $500 to the first-prize winner, $250 to the second-place kid, with $100 going to the third-place finisher. It was half those amounts for the fifth and sixth graders.

That's quite a lot of money for young kids, even now. Greg and Denny were quite excited about it. Especially Denny. He said that if he won he was going to buy some new clothes for everyone in his family. As I said, they've had a hard time. They aren't going around in rags, but they can look a bit threadbare at times. The day before the competition, Greg said to me, "Grandpa, I hope Denny beats me this year. He needs that $500 a lot more than I do." I said that even second prize would mean a lot to Denny. Greg nodded, but he had kind of a funny look in his eye.

As usual, the auditorium was packed for the competition. The crowd really gets into it, applauding every correct spelling, and groaning when a kid misses a word and drops out, with the groans followed by really big applause for the effort.

At the end of the evening, we'd got to the point where there were only three kids left in the seventh- and eighth- grade contest— Greg and Denny and an eighth-grade girl named Louise. The words were getting hard by that time. They were all flying along and then Greg got the word "apologia." I thought that would be a cinch for him, but to my astonishment, he missed it, spelling it with a double "p." Now, Greg had had a problem with the word "apology" when he was younger— he always wanted to double the "p." We all have our blind spots. Mine is "occurred." I always want to leave out the second "r." Don't ask me why. One of those things. I have to watch myself. But I thought Greg had gotten over that problem a couple of years earlier. I was just stunned, and so was the audience. They expected him to win. There was a moment of dead silence when the judge said, "I'm sorry, that's incorrect." Not even any groans, just silence. So the word passed to Louise, and she got it right. So Greg was out of the contest with only third prize. Louise and Denny went through several more words and then Denny won when Louise stumbled over "loquacious."

When Greg missed on "apologia," I saw Denny's head swivel to look at Greg. He was as surprised as everyone else. And he really looked crestfallen when Greg was eliminated. He started his next word wrong, but then caught himself, and went on to win.

I was certain Greg had misspelled "apologia" on purpose, to give Denny a chance to win. But I didn't say anything to anyone at the time. In the car on the way home, Greg said, "I don't know what happened to me there. Went back to an old mistake. Really stupid. But at least Denny got to win."

A couple of weeks later, Greg was over at the house, and we were watching the History Channel together, and there was that word,

55

"apologia." When a commercial came on I turned down the sound, and asked Greg, "Tell me something, man to man here, did you miss 'apologia' on purpose in the spelling bee?"

Greg bit his lip and lowered his eyes. Then he looked up again and said, "I can't lie to you, Grandpa. But it's got to be our secret. I really wanted Denny to win, because he needs the money so much, but I knew I had to be careful about it. There were words that I just couldn't miss on, because Denny would have known I was doing it on purpose. And I didn't want to do it at the end, when it was just him and me on the stage. 'Apologia' came along, and it was the perfect thing to screw up. There were teachers who knew I used to mess up with "apology," and you knew that, and Denny did, lots of people did. So it just worked out."

I gave my grandson a pat on the shoulder and said, "Well, Greg, in this case, I admire you for what you did—a lot. Just don't make a habit of it, okay?"

"Oh, I won't," he said. "Next year I'm going to win, you'll see."

And that's what he just did. He's off to the state championship next week. I'm very proud of him. But I'm very proud of him for misspelling "apologia" last year, too. Winning isn't everything in life. And there are different ways of winning, too.

—*Jim, 63*

A Family Talent

$\mathcal{I}$ was born, grew up, went to college, married, and raised a family right here in the great state of Maine. Wanderlust was not among my vices. Our daughter Peg is the same way, although she did try the big city once for a year right after she graduated from college. By the big city I don't mean Portland, or even Boston. No, it had to be New York. Sam, that's my husband, and I weren't too thrilled with the idea, but she had made up her mind, "New York or bust." You see, Peg is a very talented gal. She does portraits that are exceptional. She can do oils, acrylics, watercolors, pastels, or charcoals, with each medium giving a different effect. Oh, and let's not forget crayons, which is what she started out with as a child.

Her talent wasn't too big a surprise since I've been painting seascapes—using oils—since I was a teenager. Growing up on the coast of Maine provides a landscape painter with an endless source of subjects. All those crashing waves and dramatic sunsets just begging to be captured on canvas! This far north, the changes in the seasons are very noticeable, and even in the course of a mid-summer month the weather can pass through several different phases, so that the light is ever-changing. You can paint virtually the same scene a dozen times in a year and end up with twelve very distinct pictures. The coast of Maine never gets boring.

At first, I mostly gave my paintings away,

to friends and relatives. Once in a while, someone would insist on giving me twenty-five or fifty dollars, but I didn't consider myself a professional. I didn't even study art at college. I was a biology major, a subject I've put to good use working for the Maine Department of Fisheries for the last several decades. My father was a fisherman, so it was a natural career for me.

But when I was twenty-three, the year after I married Sam, a man from Tulsa, Oklahoma, who was visiting his wife's relatives in Maine, saw a couple of my pictures at a local restaurant a cousin of mine owned, and asked about them. He came around to see me, looked at some more pictures, and suggested he give me a professional show at a gallery he had attached to a framing shop in Tulsa. So I packed up a dozen pictures and sent them off, moaning about the expense and hoping I'd sell two or three and make a little profit. Three weeks later, Mr. Tulsa (which is what I call him to this day) called me long distance and said, in his wry way, "Chrissy, the show went well. I'll be sending you a check in the mail. Goodbye, dear." "Goodbye, dear," indeed. I didn't even have a chance to react or ask him how many had been sold. He must have sent the check by reverse pony express, because it took ten days to arrive. When I opened the envelope and saw the amount it was made out for, Sam had to pick me up off the floor. All twelve pictures had sold, and I'd earned more than a thousand dollars—which was a lot of money in Maine in the 1950s. Mr. Tulsa had written a short note: "Dear Girl—

Congratulations on your first professional show. It seems that no one in Oklahoma has ever seen the sea before, as I somewhat expected, and people were enthralled with your exotic views of another planet." So that was how it all began for me.

With my daughter Peg, it was different. She would have nothing to do with seascapes, or even still lifes. From the start, she drew faces. That meant she wasn't competing with me—in fact, I've never been any good at faces. Oh, I can draw them, of course, but my coastline rocks are more expressive. Peg, though, could capture not just someone's "look" but their whole personality. It always seemed a kind of magic to me.

Early on, Peg was drawing full-length portraits for a while. Sam and I were a little taken aback when she showed us one of her latest efforts, which was based on a photo in a book we had on the history of sculpture. It was Michelangelo's David. All of him. Sam mumbled something about fig leaves—Peg was only nine, after all. I just told her it was beautiful, which it was. As the years went by, however, she began to concentrate on faces. With my example to go by, she was selling her pictures by the time she was fourteen. She specialized in pictures of young children—a very smart move, financially speaking. Half the people in town wanted a portrait of their children or grandchildren. I well remember the day she came home and announced, "I got two new clients today." How many fifteen-year-olds do you know with clients?

Anyway, after college, she was determined to try her luck in New York. She had landed what seemed a good job with an advertising agency, although she quickly discovered that what had sounded like an excellent salary didn't go very far in New York. And she just hated her work. She had a special talent for getting at the very particular reality of anyone whose portrait she did, but of course what they wanted at the agency was all-purpose, generic faces that would appeal to a mass audience. She could do that, but it bored her to death. So after one year she came back home, married her childhood sweetheart, Bruce, and settled in to raise a family. After a few months she became pregnant with what she assumed would be a girl. No, "assumed" is not the right word. She was willing herself a daughter. She could have found out for certain, of course, but she didn't. Just knew she was going to have a daughter who would be named Pamela.

Naturally, it turned out to be a boy, who was named Preston instead. Sam and I were at the hospital with Bruce when Preston was born. Bruce was very happy to have a son, and Peg was at least beginning to warm up to the idea when we went in to see her, but Sam was in a great rush to get out of there. He practically dragged me out of the place. "What is the big hurry?" I asked. "Have to get to the paint store," Sam said. And so the two of us spent the next ten hours at Peg and Bruce's house repainting the nursery blue instead of pink. I got to redo the trim because of my "steady hand," as Sam put it, but which really meant that Grandma instead of Grandpa had to crawl around on the floor all day.

Preston lived up to the blue paint. He was all boy. He didn't show the slightest interest in anything artistic. Peg was really quite disappointed. When Preston was about twelve she said to me, "I can't understand it. That kid grew up breathing turpentine fumes and knocking over my easels. Where did I go wrong?"

Preston's first love was soccer, which was just catching on at the time, and he was very good at it. He had legs like tree trunks by the eighth grade. We were all proud of him, including his mother. Peg was mostly kidding when she lamented his lack of interest in art.

But then something strange happened. The summer between eighth grade and high school, a lot of Preston's friends got jobs. Mowing lawns, bagging groceries, whatever. Things change along the Maine coast in summer, with the arrival of people who have summer homes and the influx of tourists. There are lot of extra jobs around, even for kids just entering their teens. The job Preston applied for surprised us. It was all his idea—he saw an ad in the paper for a helper at the Old Wharf Puppet Theater.

This puppet theater is an institution around here, going back forty years. It's run by Ted Bracken, who was a couple of years behind me in school. He started it in his early twenties. His parents owned the general store down by the Old Wharf, which sold everything from fishing tackle to flour to dried cod. There was a space in the same building, which they owned, which was just kind of an oversized storeroom, and Ted persuaded them to let him use it as a puppet theater during the tourist season. As the years went by, he fixed it up so that it was quite a grand little place. When one of the movie theaters closed down in the 60s, he bought the seats to replace the wooden chairs he'd had before. There's a proscenium arch he constructed, and the box office inside the theater is enclosed in some nineteenth-century glass panels he picked up at a flea market.

Ted and his wife Millie ran the general store year 'round after his parents retired, adding a lot more tourist items over the years. And the puppet theater started operating more or less year 'round, too. It didn't run non-stop, but Ted would do a Halloween show, a Thanksgiving show, a Christmas show, one at Easter, and then would open every weekend from June to mid-September. He wrote the shows, including new lyrics to old songs and hymns, and he and Millie made the puppets and costumes. They did all the famous fairy tales, from "Cinderella" to "Sleeping Beauty," over the years, and things like Dickens's *A Christmas Carol* or the story of the first Pilgrim Thanksgiving.

The summer Preston got his job with Ted, a helper was needed because Millie had developed bad arthritis. Preston had seen all Ted's shows when he was little—they were aimed at kids from about four to eight, although there were always a few jokes that only parents would get. Ted and Millie didn't have any children of their own, but of course they were beloved by almost every kid in town. Still, as I said, we were a little surprised when Preston applied for the job. It was a long way from the soccer field. Even so, it became a real turning point for him.

Preston did all kinds of jobs that summer, from sweeping up to adjusting the lights that illuminated the stage. But the most important thing that happened was that Ted taught him to make the papier mâché that was used for the puppets' heads and hands. By the end of the summer he was even shaping the heads and finally painting them. Ted was amazed. "He's a real artist," he told Peg. "Better than I am." He was right. Preston could take that papier mâché glop and mold it into astonishing faces. But that was just the start.

Preston continued to work for Ted over the next several summers, but he also branched out and started making sculptures of papier mâché. I remember Peg calling up one day when he was fifteen and saying, "Preston has taken over half my studio, Mother. I hardly have room to turn around anymore." She was not really complaining, of course. Nothing could have pleased her more.

There's a gallery in town that's been showing my paintings for decades, although I've also had shows in Portland and Boston. Most of Peg's portraits are commissions, but the summer before Preston went off to college, we talked the gallery owner into giving us a three-generation show. He included my seascapes, several portraits Peg had done of well-known people, and ten of Preston's papier mâché sculptures, which ranged from a five-foot-long chili pepper to a kind of futuristic totem pole that was free-standing and eight feet high. He also had a number of smaller pieces that would sell more easily.

Half the town turned out for the opening, along with many of the people with summer homes. There was wine and good cheese and it was very festive indeed. The opening lasted from five to seven, and after the door was closed, we walked around and checked the little red stickers that indicated what had already sold. Peg and I had done very well, but every single one of Preston's pieces had sold! That included the totem pole, which had been bought by a New York couple who built a very impressive modern house here a few years ago. Preston had asked Ted and Millie Bracken to stay behind, and we poured a fresh glass of wine for everyone. Sam was there, of course, and Preston's dad. Preston raised his plastic glass and said, "I'd like to make a toast. Here's to my very talented grandmother and mother, who passed along some good genes, and to Ted Bracken, who taught me so much."

I think that's one of the nicest moments in my life. Preston's away at college now, an art major. He's learning to work in bronze, and I have a sneaking hunch that he's going to out-strip his mother and grandmother by quite a margin in the long run. I did tell him, though, that I hoped when it came to bronzes he wasn't going to be turning out any eight-foot-high totem poles, at least not right away. He grinned and said, "Oh, I think that's a year or two down the line, Grandma."

—*Chrissy, 65*

Guide My Hand

When my daughter Rachel was pregnant for the second time, she was infected with rubella, or German measles, which is harmless enough at any other time but can lead to birth defects when a pregnant woman contracts it. My granddaughter Kathy was born blind as a result. She was otherwise perfect, a lovely baby who grew into a very pretty little girl with blond hair and the most infectious smile in the world.

Rachel and her husband Hal had been fully aware there could be a birth defect, and they counted themselves lucky that it hadn't been a worse problem. A friend of theirs had given birth to a boy with Down's syndrome, a very severe case, and he had to be institutionalized. Rachel and Hal set an example of acceptance that we grandparents, on both sides, tried to emulate, but I must say it wasn't easy. Hal's mother, Virginia, and I had many long talks about the situation, and we ended up in tears more than once—not for ourselves, but for Rachel and Hal and, especially, Kathy. My husband Fred and Virginia's husband Lou tried to be stoic about it, but we knew they were upset, too.

But Rachel and Hal went about things in a wonderful way. They read everything they could find on the subject of blindness, from Milton's poem on his own blindness (which came much later in life) to Helen Keller's autobiography. They read a lot of medical material, too. But there was no hope of restoring Kathy's sight, even with eye transplants. So they simply set to work doing their very best for her. They began teaching her braille very early, and fortunately Kathy was a very bright child. It's difficult to translate the world we see into terms that a blind child can understand, at least at the beginning. You have to think differently, like explaining colors by having the child feel a series of textures. Green was easy. They got that across with grass and fresh leaves. But red was difficult. There are many different ways to go about it, but for Kathy red was finally grasped in terms of a filled hot water bottle. What works for one child doesn't necessarily do the job with another, but Rachel and Hal talked to many experts, and many parents of blind children, and they were all very helpful. Still, it's a trial-and-error process, and you have to have great patience, and not push too hard if things aren't going well.

As a grandparent, watching the process was sometimes frustrating and anxiety provoking, but as time went on we learned to take great joy in the successes and to realize that there were more to come. One of the things that encouraged us all was the part that Kathy's older brother David played in helping his sister to take her place in the world. He was almost six when Kathy was born, old enough to understand the situation. It was wonderful to watch him with her. He was terrific with her from the start, and as he got older, he was the one who made many learning breakthroughs with her. He was still enough of a child himself at nine or ten to be able to figure out ways of getting through to Kathy that might not have occurred to an adult.

I think watching David play with Kathy and instinctively teaching her about the world as he did, was one of the most fascinating—and often moving—things I've ever seen. I remember him sitting on the floor of my kitchen teaching Kathy to use fingerpaints, guiding her hand, taking her little fingers and dipping them into the paint, telling her the color, and then gently pulling her fingers across the paper making designs. Kathy's been using fingerpaints ever since, doing wonderful things. Her paintings were even put in student shows, and if people didn't know her background, they'd never guess they were done by a blind person. They aren't figurative, of course, but they have truly lovely, evocative patterns, the kind nature makes. I couldn't do it for beans—I've tried.

One thing that was lucky for Kathy was that her family lived in Boston. Her father teaches at M.I.T. My husband and I live in Brookline, just next door, as it were. Hal grew up in Indiana, where his parents still are, although they come East for a visit at least twice a year. Being in Boston meant that it was very convenient for Kathy to go to the Perkins School for the Blind. That's where Annie Sullivan went before she was hired to teach Helen Keller, of course, and it's an extraordinary place. It's not just the expertise the instructors have, which is astonishing in itself, but also the atmosphere they create. It's a joyous place where there's a small triumph several times a day. At the same time there's a strong sense of discipline. The object is to teach young people how to become self-sufficient, so that they can make their own way in the world.

When Kathy turned thirteen, she got her first Seeing Eye dog. Rachel and Hal had an Irish setter when Kathy was born, Maggie, who was a lovely, sweet dog, and the two grew up together. When Maggie died, Kathy's parents decided it was time for her to have her own special companion. Getting a Seeing Eye dog isn't just a matter of picking one out and going home with it, of course. The dogs go through a long training process, and then the owner has to be trained, too. Kathy's dog was a German shepherd, as so many Seeing Eye dogs are. They're extremely loyal, and they have an extraordinary instinct for keeping their owners out of harm's way. Kathy's dog was a female, and she called her Annie, after Annie Sullivan. All parents and grandparents have nervous moments when a child starts going out into the world on her own, and with a blind child the fears are compounded. But it helps when the child has the likes of Annie going with her. I said to Rachel once that I wouldn't have been surprised to see Annie get up on her hind legs and carry an umbrella, like Mary Poppins.

I've said that Kathy was very bright, and all of us hoped that she could go on to college. But that's a massive undertaking for a blind person. Braille is a wonderful thing, but if you're going to get a college degree, you have to deal with all kinds of research for which no braille text exists. Fred and I and Rachel and Hal all took turns reading aloud to Kathy, of course, and the growth in the number of recordings of books helped, too. But it still required a small army of volunteers to help her through. We knew a young man who'd just gotten through Harvard Law with that kind of help, and Kathy said that if Gordon could cope with Harvard Law, she could certainly get an undergraduate degree. Along with people who teach illiterate adults to read, I think the volunteers who read to the blind are among the best people in the world.

So Kathy went to Wellesley College, just outside of Boston, where Hillary Rodham Clinton went. It has a beautiful campus that's pretty much self-contained, which made it easier for Kathy to navigate than Harvard, in the middle of Cambridge. Aside from the work load, college can present new problems for blind people. Kathy was used to teachers who were specialists in working with the blind. College professors who've never had a blind student in class can react strangely. Some can be overly solicitous, in ways that are unintentionally condescending. At the other extreme, you'll find some who are impatient, with a kind of "Why me?" attitude. Not that anyone was nasty, but it took some adjustments on Kathy's part and on the part of her teachers, too. In another sense, of course, all this was to the good in terms of Kathy's future. The danger of going to a specialized school like Perkins is in being overprotected. The real world is somewhat rougher.

But Kathy more than adjusted. She graduated last spring with honors in English. For her parents, for Fred and me, and for Virginia and Lou, who had come from Indiana for the occasion, it was a very proud day indeed. David, who had graduated from Harvard five years earlier, traveled all the way from California to be with his sister. Because of complicated business negotiations he was involved with, it wasn't certain he'd be able to make it, and he told Kathy he probably couldn't, so she wouldn't be counting on him too much. But at the last minute he was able to get the red-eye east. We all cried when Kathy was handed her diploma, but the best moment came afterward, when she joined us on the lawn. Each one of us embraced her, first her two grandmothers, then her grandfathers, and then her parents. And then, before David could say anything or step forward, Kathy reached out toward him and said, "I know you're there, David. Guide my hand."

—*Connie, 72*

4

they were very brave

Courage is a quality we hope to discover in ourselves when the need arises. Parents look for it in their children. Its presence is reassuring, a sign that a child will be able to cope with dangers and setbacks that all human beings must confront at one time or another. But the bravery of a grandchild often carries an additional degree of meaning. To see a grandchild rise to the occasion and deal with a crisis, or overcome an affliction, gives grandparents a special sense of continuity, providing a reaffirmation of the value of being alive and meeting the inevitable challenges of life. When a grandchild shows courage, it serves to sharpen the sense that the human will to cope, to go on, to prevail, can be sustained not just in the present but through successive generations. To tell the story of a grandchild's bravery conveys a message that transcends simple family pride— it speaks to all our brave moments, past, present and future, over the rolling years.

There are many kinds of bravery, of course. It can be shown in situations that threaten life itself, or in quieter ways in far more domestic circumstances. Sometimes bravery is a matter of coping not just with an immediate crisis but of sustaining that kind of courage for a lifetime. It can simply be a question of taking a bad situation and turning it into something else. The stories told by the grandparents in this chapter

71

range across all these possibilities. You will meet a grandfather who takes justifiable pride in a grandson's adapting to what most people would regard as a catastrophe; and a grandmother who plays a central role in helping her granddaughter to make the best of an even worse contingency. There is also a little girl who, with a calm and sense beyond her years, saves herself and her grandmother from a frightening situation. Another grandmother tells of how her teenage grandson dealt with a more domestic crisis that involved the courage to make a very grown-up and generous decision. And a grandfather celebrates a gifted athlete's ability to turn a serious setback into a plan for the future.

The grandparents telling these stories are very proud of their grandchildren, and they have every right to be.

The Church Bells in the Fog

My son Mike and his wife Jackie rent a house for a month every summer on Cape Cod. It's in a small village, East Dennis, that hasn't been developed the way most of the Cape has. They still pay a pretty penny to rent the house, too much in my opinion, but they can afford it, I guess, and their two children just love it there. My granddaughter Sarah is eleven, and my grandson Dale is seven. Dale is named after my husband, who was a dozen years older than me. We would always drive up to visit Mike and his family on the Cape for a long weekend, but Dale passed away last winter, and this past summer Mike and Jackie asked me to spend the whole month with them. That was just what I needed, and I was very grateful to them.

East Dennis has only about thirty houses, and a lovely white New England church in the middle of it, with a pointed steeple on top of a square bell tower. The house Mike and Jackie rent every year is a good-sized Victorian with a big porch on two sides. It's got a wonderful big kitchen, where we ate most of our meals. You can walk to the beach from the house—it doesn't take more than about five minutes, down a hill to the sand dunes. There's a parking lot, but you have to have a permit to park there, so there aren't many tourists. On a weekday afternoon, even in the middle of August, it can be almost deserted. The beach has lovely white sand, and there's a stone breakwater that separates it from a cozy little harbor. Sarah and Dale loved to climb around on that breakwater.

It's also a very good beach for shell-gathering, at least when the tide is low, and especially after a storm. Sarah has quite a collection she's gathered there, including a number of starfish and sand dollars.

There was a storm in the middle of August, and there was to be a very low tide late the next afternoon, so Sarah wanted to go looking for more shells. Mike and Jackie wanted to drive across the Cape to Chatham that day, to buy some fresh fish at the docks where the fishing boats come in there, and Dale decided to go with them while Sarah and I went shell-hunting on the beach. It was a hazy afternoon, and when we got down to the beach at about four o'clock the last few beachgoers were just leaving. Sarah and I had the sand bars all to ourselves.

The tide goes out more than a hundred yards there, when it's really low, and Sarah and I went out quite a way. The sand bars had a wonderful feeling to them, hard and soft at the same time, very nice on the feet. And there were lots of little rivulets to wade through, between the raised areas of sand. Sarah had a bucket she was filling up with shells, and I took off my bathing cap and started piling small shells into that. We were concentrating so hard on the sand, trying to spot shells that were dug in a bit, that we'd hardly looked up in several minutes. And when we did, we realized that we were surrounded by fog. It had rolled in very suddenly. I could just see Sarah and she was only about ten feet away, and by the time I had walked over to her, the fog had thickened to the point that you couldn't even see your hand if you held your arm out full length in front of you.

I was quite alarmed, to tell you the truth. I took Sarah's hand and we stood there silently for a moment, trying to see around us.

"Do you know which way the beach is?" I asked Sarah.

"I'm not sure, Grandma," she said. "I was turning around a lot."

"Oh, Lord," I said. What worried me was that when the tide turned it came in very quickly. There were a number of higher spots on the sand bars, and if we were on one of those, the tide could come in around us, leaving us on an island. That would put water on both sides of us, and if we started swimming, we could just as easily be swimming out to sea as toward the shore.

"Don't worry, Grandma," Sarah said, squeezing my hand. "We'll just wait for the church bells."

I gave a strangled kind of laugh at that. I'd always complained about the church bells when my husband Dale and I came up in the past. They rang every fifteen minutes, and it was always hard for me to sleep the first night. You get used to them soon enough, of course, but they can be irritating at first.

"They rang just a couple of minutes ago, didn't they?" I asked. In fact, it was the sound of the bells that had made me look up and see the fog around us.

"Yes, Grandma," Sarah said, very matter-of-factly. "We'll have to wait a while."

A while. Well, twelve or thirteen minutes may seem like a little while under most circumstances, but standing there in the fog, it seemed like an eternity. In a very short time, I felt water lapping at my ankles, and I started to become really frightened. "Don't you think we should decide where we think the shore is and start moving toward it? We should be able to tell quite quickly if we're on the right track."

"No," Sarah said. "We have to stay right where we are until we hear the bells."

"I guess you're right," I said. Then, trying to buck myself up as much as Sarah, I said, "Well, why don't we tell some jokes to pass the time." Sarah and I both like jokes, the sillier the better.

But Sarah said that we couldn't do that. "We have to keep quiet and listen for the bells."

I knew she was right, of course, but my heart was just racing along. Sarah put an arm around my waist and I put my arm over her shoulder. She seemed so calm, and I thought about what a splendid girl she was. That made me feel better and I calmed down a little. But I have to say that the next ten minutes or so seemed the longest I've ever experienced.

And then the sound of the bells finally came. They sounded far away, muffled by the fog, I guess, not making that racket I was always so aware of when I first arrived. But it was clear which direction they were coming from. They were behind us. If we had started walking, we would have been heading out to sea.

We turned around and walked toward the bells, hand in hand. At one point the water was above my knees, and up to Sarah's chest, where the water had rushed in to a gully in the sand. But we didn't have to actually swim. The bells stopped ringing before we were safe, but we knew we were going in the right direction, and soon enough we were back on the beach. The fog wasn't quite as thick there, and we walked up over the dunes and into the parking lot, and found the road back up to the village.

We got back home before the rest of the family. There was fog around the house too, but not terribly thick. We heard the car, and saw its headlights.

The minute the engine stopped, we heard my son's voice calling, "Mother? Sarah?"

Sarah and I were out on the porch by then. "Here we are," we both called out.

Mike and Jackie and Dale all came rushing up onto the porch and hugged us. Mike said, "When we got back to this side of the Cape and saw the fog, I was very worried about you two, but Jackie said, 'Don't underestimate your daughter,' and of course she was right."

I said, "Truer words were never spoken," and we told about our adventure in the fog. Of course Dale had to claim that he would have known what to do, too. Sarah just smiled. I don't think she even felt she'd been particularly brave or smart, just sensible. But I was very proud of her. And when I think about it now, I'm even a little bit proud of myself. I was quite frightened out there on the sand bars with the water coming in and not being able to see two feet in front of me, but at least I had the sense to shut up and trust my grand-daughter. Sometimes an eleven-year-old is much wiser than Grandma.

—*Nan, 67*

Speed on Crutches

I've got three grandsons, and they're all fine boys, but my daughter Carolyn's son Tom is a really remarkable kid. He was hit by a truck while riding his bicycle when he was ten, and his left leg was so badly fractured they had to amputate it. That was six years ago. These days, of course, they can do wonders with prosthetic limbs, but he decided that he wanted to wait until he was full grown before getting an artificial leg. Otherwise, you have to go through a whole series of legs as you get taller, and he didn't want to be bothered with that. It was completely his decision. I was dubious about it at first, but he proved me wrong.

Once, thirty years ago, I had a broken leg and had to be on crutches for a few weeks, and I found them very awkward. But Tom was incredible with them. When he really got going, anyone who wanted to keep up with him had to jog—you couldn't do it just walking. And stairs were no problem for him, going up or down. He has an uncanny sense of timing and balance. Obviously, he was a born athlete, and at first I thought it was awfully sad that he'd never be able to capitalize on that. But I was wrong again. He's on his high school swim team, and not because of any special treatment, either. He wins races. Part of that is because using crutches developed his shoulders and arms terrifically. His upper body is extremely strong. A year ago I was talking with him about his swimming, and I admitted that his crutches had actually been a benefit in giving him upper-body strength. He grinned at me and said, "Well, that's true, Grandad, but I've got another advantage, too—less weight to pull through water."

That's what I like about him most, I think—his ability to look at what most of us see as a devastating handicap as something that might even have its positive side. Of course, if he had both legs and could get that extra kick, he'd be even faster in the water. But he refuses to look at it that way. My wife Sarah was a nurse for many years, working in veteran's hospitals, and she says that developing that kind of attitude was often the toughest challenge many amputees faced. So often they could only see the loss. Maybe Tom was lucky that it happened to him when he was so young, perhaps young kids have more resilience. But I'm not so sure about that. I think it has something to do with personality, or character.

Tom's very bright, as well. Straight A's. There's no question he's headed for a top college. There is some question about when he's going to get an artificial leg, though. The plan was for him to do it the summer between high school and college. That would give him a while to get used to it before he starts in with a whole new phase of his life. But I'm not sure he wants to do that now. He's so tremendously mobile on crutches that he's concerned an artificial leg would really slow him down. He recognizes that there would be advantages to getting rid of them, but he feels that he'd like to start college on his crutches, which he's so secure with, and get to know new people on that basis before switching over to an artificial leg. I can understand that in a way. But I'll tell you this—whatever he decides to do, I'll back him up. Tom has more sense about what's good for him than a lot of adults I know. I trust him completely to make the right decision.

—*Jake, 63*

A Veterinary Emergency

I have two cats. One is an old lady, like me, and she's called Matilda, after my favorite great aunt when I was a child a thousand years ago. The other is a young fellow, only four years old, black and white with an extremely intelligent face. His name is Aladdin. Now, Matilda has a great deal of dignity, and tends to be snooty with strangers, or even with people she knows well if they happen to be somebody she thinks beneath her notice. Aladdin is just the opposite, very friendly and sweet with everyone. He likes to jump on top of things, like my bureau, and I'll lean over and put my face right in front of his and we'll rub foreheads. I've had cats all my life, but I must say Aladdin is my absolute favorite. Matilda knows this, of course, animals always do, but she's really quite decent about it—she never was in the forehead-rubbing business anyway.

Last spring I went on a ten-day cruise to the Caribbean with my old friend Louisa. We're both widows but neither of us is the kind to let life pass us by, and we often take short trips together. While I was away, my grandson Gary came over to feed Matilda and Aladdin once a day. He's the youngest of my seven grandchildren, and was fifteen at the time. I have two daughters and a son, and although both the daughters live halfway across the country, my son lives about a dozen blocks from me in Lancaster, Pennsylvania. He and Allie have two grown children who are already out in the world. Gary was something of a late surprise, but a very welcome one. He's the kind of boy every parent might wish for, if I do say so. You'll see what I mean.

As it happened, his father and mother were going to be away themselves for the second weekend of my cruise, which would leave Gary completely on his own. But nobody worried about that. He's very resourceful— and it turned out that he needed to be. When he bicycled over to feed the cats on that second Saturday, Matilda was waiting for him right inside the front door, which was very unlike her. She started mewing away and seemed very nervous, and he found out why as soon as he went into the kitchen. Aladdin was lying on the kitchen floor, practically comatose. When Gary petted his head, he opened his eyes but otherwise he didn't move. It was obvious that something was very wrong.

Gary had the number of my vet and called there immediately, but they close at two o'clock on Saturday, and it was already four. The recorded message gave the number of the emergency animal hospital, so Gary called there and told the assistant what was going on. She said that he should bring Aladdin in right away. Well, with his parents away, Gary had to figure out how to get Aladdin to the emergency animal shelter. He knew it was only about twenty blocks, but he didn't think Aladdin should be subjected to a rough bicycle ride. So he telephoned Mark, his next-door neighbor who's seventeen and has his license, and asked if he could help. Mark said he could drive Gary there but he couldn't wait, because he had a date at six and he hadn't showered or anything. Gary said fine, just get them there fast.

He got the carry-case out of the cellar and put Aladdin in it as gently as he could, but even so the poor thing cried out in pain. When they got to the animal hospital, the young woman Gary had talked to on the phone took one look at Aladdin and carried him in to one of the two vets on duty. About five minutes later, the vet came out and explained the situation to Gary. He said that Aladdin's urethra was blocked— something that's common enough in male cats, but very serious. He asked Gary if he'd noticed Aladdin having any trouble urinating, and Gary had to explain that it was my cat, and that even though he cleaned up the litter every day, with two cats using the same box it was hard to tell about something like that.

The vet looked a little disturbed at the news that it wasn't Gary's cat. He said that he thought Aladdin could be saved, but that it was going to cost about five hundred dollars for the procedures and the three nights at the hospital—Monday was Memorial Day, and Aladdin's regular vet wouldn't be open until Tuesday, he knew. Even then, Aladdin would have to be transferred to the regular vet for another two or three days' care. So he thought Gary should call his parents and see if it was all right to spend that kind of money. Well, of course Gary's parents were away, and he doubted if he could reach them until late that night, and there I was cruising the Caribbean. A decision had to be made right away, though, if Aladdin's life was going to be saved.

Gary didn't hesitate. He said to go ahead and do anything that was necessary.

The vet was very nice, but he wondered if Gary really had the "authority" to make a decision involving that much money.

Gary said that he thought it was what I would want him to do, but if he was wrong, he'd pay for it himself. He explained that he was saving money to buy an old car to fix up when he turned sixteen next year, and he had about a thousand dollars. "That should cover it, right?" he asked. The vet smiled and said that would certainly do it.

I talked to the vet myself after I got home, to thank him for saving Aladdin, and he said, "Well, ma'am, I just did my job. What your grandson did was above and beyond the call of duty. He's really the one who saved Aladdin. He's quite a kid. Young man, I should say."

Well, he didn't have to tell me that. I'd always known it, and if I hadn't, Gary would certainly have proved it that weekend.

Aladdin recovered fully, I'm happy to say. And when we're busy rubbing foreheads, I often think that he wouldn't be here if it wasn't for my very grown-up, and very unselfish grandson.

—*Dorothy, 76*

Knees

My daughter Rosemary and her husband Bill had three kids. As grandparents, Doris and I thought they were all terrific, of course, but since we hadn't had a son ourselves, I took kind of a special interest in my grandson Vince, and not just because he was named after me. All three of them are grown now. Lois, the oldest, was always very musical, and she works for Columbia Records. Betty was more introspective and became a librarian. Vince is the youngest, and from early on it was clear that he had extraordinary athletic ability. Where he got it from it's hard to say. Doris and I both played golf, but with big handicaps. Rosemary was a good swimmer and played a lot of tennis, but just for recreation. On Bill's side of the family, there wasn't much athleticism, either, except of the couch-potato kind. I did have an uncle who made the Olympic track team back in 1908. Maybe that's where it came from. Genes can be funny that way.

In high school, Vince played both baseball and football, and was the team standout in both sports. He played center field on the baseball team, hit for a high average, and could easily steal bases since he ran like a jackrabbit. On the football team he was a wide receiver, and once he got his hands on the ball, he was gone. In his junior year, his baseball team won the state championship, and the football team came close, but the quarterback, who was a senior, had a very serious knee injury. When that happened, I thought to myself, "That could have been Vince." There's a lot of glory in high school and college sports, but so many kids get injured. I guess some parents and grandparents think it can't happen to their kid or grandkid, but it always worried me.

During Vince's senior year in high school there were a lot of colleges trying to recruit him, he was that good. He had an offer from the Minnesota Twins on the baseball side, too, to play in their farm system. But he turned that down flat. He was a fine athlete, but he also had a head on his shoulders and wanted to go to college. He went to the University of Minnesota—we were from St. Paul—where he got an excellent scholarship. They wanted him to concentrate on football and forget about baseball, and he agreed. At the college level, that's a much bigger sport than baseball, of course.

In his sophomore year, he began as the number three wide receiver, and was seriously challenging the two seniors ahead of him. He was majoring in biology. His dad was a dentist, and Vince had serious thoughts about going into medicine. But it was beginning to look as though he might even have a pro career in football. By the end of his sophomore season, he was a starter, and scoring touchdowns in a big way. The pro scouts started mentioning his name, and that buzz got going that you hear every year on televised college games.

Vince was very level-headed about it all. There were still two years of college football ahead of him, and he pointed out that there were a number of hotshot wide receivers across the country. He loved the game, but he wasn't the kind of boy to put all his eggs into one basket. Scholastically, he was on the honor roll, and he intended to stay there. Thank God that was his attitude. In the first game of his junior season, he was tackled by two guys coming at him from opposite sides. Doris and I were there along with his parents, and the minute he went down, we knew he was badly hurt. It was his right knee. The cartilage was torn every which way. I thought about Zach, the quarterback on his high school team, who'd never played again. He and Vince had been close, and Vince had felt very badly for him. That knee injury was a real tragedy for Zach. He came from a poor family, and his athletic ability had been his ticket to something better. He'd been a bright kid—good quarterbacks have to be—and he still managed to get into college, but then his father became ill, and he dropped out to become a car salesman. He's done okay, I guess, but his chances for a lot more had gone with his knee.

Vince didn't play again, either. There were two operations, and on the whole they were successful. He could run, but the speed was gone. He'd had a hunch about that the minute he went down. When we went to see him in the hospital, he'd looked up at us and kind of grinned, and said, "Well, folks, it looks like there's been a slight change of plans."

Of course, we immediately started saying he'd be back like new in no time, the things families say at times like that. He said, "I'll give it a try, but somehow I don't think so. And I've made a decision. I'm going to switch to full pre-med, and work my ass off."

We thought that was great and told him so. "Something else," he said. "I want to be a specialist. An orthopedic surgeon." This time he really grinned. I got it right away. "Knees?" I asked. "You got it, Grandad," Vince said. "For Zach and me and a whole lot of others to come."

He graduated from medical school last spring. Now, I suppose a lot of grandfathers would give almost anything to be able to turn on the television on a fall Sunday and watch their grandson play for the Packers or the Cowboys, carrying the ball into the end zone after a 39-yard reception. I would have been boasting all over the place, I'm sure. But I have to say that I do a good deal of boasting about my namesake grandson who's on his way to repairing other people's knees, making sure they walk straight and tall. With all the new surgical techniques they have these days, I have no doubt that someday he'll put some quarterback or wide receiver back together well enough so they can continue to play. And when he does, Vince will know what it means. I was very proud of my grandson when he was making touchdowns, but I think what he's decided to do with his life may count for more in the long run. There are a lot of different ways a man can be proud of his grandson.

—*Vincent, 73*

Freedom on Horseback

To start with, I should tell you that I grew up on a family farm. That's a hard life, but it does have its benefits. You certainly learn responsibility early, and the value of cooperation and hard work. But I knew the first time I went to a big city—Chicago—that I was a city girl at heart. I went to college, and got a job in advertising in New York City, where I still live. I got married in my late twenties. Rob was an editor at a publishing house that specialized in textbooks. We had a son, Bobby.

One of the few things I missed about farm life was riding horseback. I loved that as a girl. It gave me such a wonderful sense of freedom to ride out over the fields at sunset, with the tops of the trees still bright green, but shadows all along the sides of meadows below them. It was magical. Of course, I didn't get to ride very often as an adult. Rob and I made a good living, but New York is a very expensive city, and renting a horse to ride in Central Park was a real extravagance. And Bobby never learned to ride. My parents had sold the farm before I got married, so even when we visited them, there were no longer any horses to ride.

Bobby joined a Wall Street firm right out of college, and rose fast, making a lot of money. He married a wonderful girl, Melissa, and they led an almost charmed life for quite a while. Bobby had discovered skiing when he was at Dartmouth College, and Melissa was a skier, too. They had two children, a boy named Jonathan and a girl called Lisa, and as soon as the children were old enough, they taught them to ski. Every winter they'd fly out to Aspen for a skiing vacation. And they were able to do some skiing on weekends in Connecticut, where they lived. They'd go to the western part of the state, where there were some decent runs, although nothing like Aspen.

Lisa turned out to be a very fine skier, and she started to work on more and more difficult slopes when they went to Aspen. She had it in her mind to make the U.S. ski team someday. But ten years ago, when she was thirteen, she took a terrible fall. She'd fallen many times before, of course, all skiers do, and she'd broken a leg once. But this was one of those freak accidents. Her left ski didn't come loose and she got tangled up and flew about twenty feet through the air at the end of the fall. She broke her back, and the spinal injury was so severe that she was never able to walk again, let alone ski.

Lisa had always had great courage, as well as a wonderful sense of humor, and she seemed like the kind of person who would adapt to her handicap as well as you could expect anyone to. But the accident seemed to break her personality, not just her body. She was very depressed, sullen, and often self-pitying. Of course, Bobby and Melissa saw to it that she got the best treatment, psychological as well as physical, but nothing seemed to help. We were all terribly worried about her.

Then I had an idea. Even though I almost never went riding myself, I always went to the horse show at Madison Square Garden, and to big races like the Belmont Stakes, and I subscribed to a magazine about horses. So I knew what was going on in that world. I'd read about therapeutic riding more than once. There are programs for therapeutic riding in many states, and some states have several. These programs specialize in helping people with various disabilities get some exercise, and more important, to achieve a new outlook on life. They have experience with a wide range of disabilities, from people with multiple sclerosis to kids with Down's syndrome.

I thought this might be just the thing for Lisa. But grandparents have to be careful about seeming to interfere, especially in situations that are already stressful. And Melissa had become extremely protective of Lisa—to the point, both Rob and I thought, that she was making things worse. So I simply mentioned the idea of therapeutic riding to my son, quite casually. Bobby was immediately interested, and asked me a lot of questions. But he told me that it could be a problem. Melissa would probably think that was too much for Lisa to handle, and Lisa herself might resist.

As it happened, there was a therapeutic riding program just fifteen miles from where they lived in Connecticut. It took some persuading, but Melissa finally agreed to go with me to see what they were doing. I took the train out from New York, and Melissa and I drove over to check things out. The place was everything I knew it would be—on my own, I'd visited it earlier, although I didn't tell even Bobby that I'd done that. It was a lovely spot in the country, beautifully kept. The horses were just beautiful, the picture of health, and they'd all been specially trained, as were counselors. Not only were they adept with horses, but they had training in either physical therapy or psychological counseling, sometimes both.

Melissa had been very tense on the drive over, and at one point she had said, "I hope you understand, Barbara, that I'm very dubious about this. I won't be pushed into it. Don't try to lecture me. Just let me look around and see what I think for myself." And I said, "Of course, I understand that."

But after we'd been there about ten minutes, I could see Melissa starting to relax. Her shoulders literally unbunched. It wasn't just that the place was so beautifully run, and that everyone was so very pleasant and understanding. It was the looks on the faces of the handicapped riders, especially the children, that did it. There was one girl about fifteen, just a little older than Melissa, who was a quadriplegic. The gentleness and swiftness with which the counselors got her up on a horse was truly amazing. There were straps to hold her in place, and a counselor walked beside the horse while she was on it, keeping a hand on her waist at all times. And the expression on the girl's face was so wonderful you could hardly keep from crying. It wasn't just her smile. There was a kind of triumph to her expression, a sense of well-being that was astonishing.

Melissa became a convert that afternoon.

Now we had to get Lisa interested. And that was my job. We had a special relationship, the sort that grandmothers and granddaughters sometimes can have, with shared secrets from Mom and Dad. I'd taken her to the horse show once, but she was already into skiing by then, and I think the lack of speed dampened her interest. She liked going to the races better, because that fit into her dreams of being on the U.S. ski team, being the fastest down the course. But she'd never been on a horse. I'd tried to interest her, but it hadn't taken hold somehow.

So I wasn't too surprised when she reacted badly at first after I explained about therapeutic riding. I used the word "therapeutic" right from the start. It wasn't going to work to try to fool her about the kind of atmosphere she'd be in. But even though I expected resistance, I was a bit shocked by the way it came out of her. "Oh, terrific," she said with obvious sarcasm. "That's just what I need. Let's have Lisa play with the spastics and retards."

I tried to keep my voice even, but I'm sure it must have trembled a little. I said, "Well, Lisa, it's true a number of people who go there are a lot worse off than you are, but I must say you've got them all beat in the self-pity department."

Lisa stared at me as though I'd slapped her. And then she began to cry. She didn't make a sound, but the tears started rolling down her cheeks. And then she reached out and took my hand and said, "Oh, Grandma, I'll do anything you want me to."

So we made an appointment. Lisa was very quiet on the drive over, and snapped at her mother when Melissa asked if she was all right. One of the smart things about that program was that once you arrived with a new participant, they didn't keep you waiting around. They got right down to the business of getting Lisa up on a horse. Melissa and I watched from the other side of the corral fence. When Lisa was first on the horse, her face was almost expressionless, as though she was trying to keep all emotion at arm's length. But by the time the horse had been walked twice around the corral, she was smiling, and there was just a hint in her eyes of a kind of sparkle we hadn't seen in fourteen months. Melissa grabbed my hand and held it tight and said, "Thank you, Barbara, thank you *so* much." She didn't even look at me as she said that, and she told me later that she was afraid she'd cry if she did.

Lisa was riding on her own within a month, and she's been riding at least twice a week ever since. She's getting her master's degree in psychology now, and she's engaged to be married. I'm very proud of her. But the thing I treasure most is a card Lisa sent me a year to the day from the first time she got up on a horse. The card had a painting by the great English painter of horses, George Stubbs, and on the inside it said, "Thank you, Grandma, for giving me back my sense of freedom."

—*Barbara, 68*

5

how fast they grow

Parents have been known to wonder if the "terrible twos" will ever pass, and to wish that the teenage years could be considerably condensed. They also, especially in the somewhat frantic times we live in, often have the opposite feeling, regretting that time can't be slowed down so that they could spend more time with their children. But it is grandparents who have the keenest sense of the passing of time, as they approach retirement or cope with the physical limitations gradually imposed by age. If parents can sometimes be heard to note how fast their children have grown, that perception is even sharper with grandparents watching their grandchildren mature. That's particularly true, of course, for those grandparents who see their grandchildren only occasionally. If a year goes by between visits, the simple change in a grandchild's height can be astonishing, and if two years go by, the grandchild can sometimes seem to be almost a different person. Even for grandparents who live in the same town or city, and see their grandchildren on a regular basis, the changes that occur can seem unnervingly rapid.

As they watch their grandchildren grow, grandparents may sometimes have a wider range of reactions than a child's parents. In this chapter you will meet a grandmother who is amused at the relationship between two granddaughters in a way that might not be possible if she were in the middle of the situation. A grandfather discovers to his delight that his grandson has been paying very close attention to the stories he has been told about Grandad's favorite dogs. Another grandfather finds himself presented with an opportunity to air an old grievance about how his grandson was treated when he was very young. A grandmother recounts, with some pride and a little bemusement, how her grandson deals with a tricky matter of teenage protocol. And then there is a story about how a grandparent can become the pupil, and the grandchild the teacher, a role reversal that takes place even though the teacher is only twelve years old.

A Dog Story

All my life I've been a dog person. Don't get me wrong here, I don't hate cats—I've met some very nice ones. But I think dogs are much more interesting and much more responsive. My first canine friend was a present from my dad when I was about seven. "He's your responsibility, son. You take good care of the little critter." I was the happiest kid in the world with my brand-new bundle of brown fur. He was just eight weeks old, and he had big brown eyes. Since my dad had brought him home, he thought he had a right to name him. "He's called Brownie," I was told. That wasn't what I would have called him, but I didn't let on. Brownie. How corny can you get? I would have named him something interesting, like Roy, after Roy Rogers, or Hans, after *Hans Brinker*, which I'd just read. But I had my own dog and that was enough for me.

I managed to housebreak Brownie in record time. Even my Dad was impressed. If he started to do anything, I just picked him up and ran with him to the back door, even if he was dribbling on my legs—and it was summer, so I was wearing shorts all the time. He got the idea very fast. I taught him to catch a Frisbee in mid-air, which my friends thought was pretty amazing. There was this one kid I didn't get along with. His name was Max, and he was a bully. He tried to teach his dog to catch a Frisbee, and it was a complete flop. I really enjoyed that.

Brownie lived to be fourteen. As sad as I was to lose him, it was a good time for him to go. I'd gone to college just a couple of hours from where we lived, so I got home to see my parents and Brownie quite often. I brought friends along many times, especially on holidays like Thanksgiving and Easter. A lot of my classmates were from other states and couldn't afford to get home except for Christmas, and Mom was always happy to cook up a feast for them. They all thought Brownie was terrific, except for one girl I was quite serious about. She had a phobia about dogs because of a bad experience when she was little. I must say that put kind of a crimp in our relationship. Right after college I went into the Army. Vietnam. I had a low draft number and decided to join up before I got called. Brownie died just before I was inducted. As

I say, that was just as well, because I wouldn't have seen him again for two years, and he was getting awfully feeble.

I got back from Vietnam in one piece, and the first thing I did was get a new dog. I found her at an animal shelter, just a puppy, a mix of Border collie and terrier. She grew up looking mostly like a Border collie, black and white with the long fluffy tail they have, but there were some brown patches from the terrier. I called her Zelda, thinking of Zelda Fitzgerald, I guess, but mostly because I wanted an exotic name to make up for Brownie. My dad just shook his head when he heard the name.

Zelda was as smart as they come. I know, everyone says that about their dogs, but she really was. She had a lot of rubber squeak toys and I taught her the names of all of them—hamburger, hot dog, lamb chop, and so on. You could ask her to bring you one and she'd go find it, even if it was under a bed in another room. But she really proved herself when I was in my second year of graduate school. I got very ill with the flu, as sick as I've ever been in my life. It was all I could do to walk her twice a day. The rest of the time I was flat on my back in bed. The first morning I was sick, she went to the basket she slept in, dragged out the blanket, and pulled it across the room to the side of my bed. She wrapped herself up it, and unless she was eating, or I was staggering out to take her for a walk, she spent the next four days by my bed. When I got better, she pulled her blanket back over to her basket. I was really touched by that—I must have told the story a hundred times.

I got married at twenty-seven to my wife Mary, and she was a dog person, too. Zelda lived to be fourteen, and then we got another dog for our kids, Becky and Ed, another mutt—or American domestic, as I prefer to call mutts—who had some collie and some Labrador and Lord knows what else. I let the kids name him, of course. They chose Ringo, which went well with his happy, goofy nature. My son Ed, who lives out on the West Coast now, has two kids and two dogs, keeping up the family tradition. But Becky married a man who was great in every way but with one failing—he was a cat person. He had two when they were married, and they got another one when the older of those two died. They live only about an hour away, so Mary and I get to see our grandson Davy all the time. We have a dog of course, named Peggy, for Peggy Lee. I'm not sure the legendary Ms. Lee would appreciate that, since Peggy is not exactly a glamorous creature, but she has a great soul. Davy got to know Peggy well, and I told him all my dog stories. So of course he wanted his own dog. Becky and her husband Ron discouraged that, with all the usual stuff about how dogs and cats don't get along. But I finally talked them into letting me get Davy a dog for his ninth birthday.

We went to the animal shelter together so he could pick out the dog he wanted. There'd been a picture in the paper of a group of really cute puppies, and I thought he might pick one of them. But he insisted on going around the whole place and looking at every dog there. There was one cage that had an older dog in it—four years old, it turned out. She was lying at the back of the cage looking pretty forlorn. She had a kind of frowzy coat, even though she'd been bathed. Not the kind of dog people rush to adopt. But Davy looked in the cage and said, "Hi, there." Her ears pricked up immediately and she lifted her head and looked at Davy. Frowzy coat or no, she had absolutely beautiful brown eyes. And she gave Davy what I can only describe as "the look."

A lot of dog experts say that kids should always be allowed to pick out their own dogs, because it isn't just the kid choosing the dog. The dog sometimes chooses the kid. Well, I could see right away that Davy had just been chosen. "That's her!" Davy said. "That's Dazzle!" I'd seldom seen a less dazzling dog in my life, except for those eyes, but I didn't say anything. I was a little worried that an older dog might be a problem with cats, but the nice young woman who was in charge said that the dog had in fact grown up with a cat. The owner had been an elderly widow who was now in a nursing home. I asked if they knew the dog's name, since it's not really a good idea to change an older dog's name. The young woman said it had been Frazzle. It was quite appropriate. The old lady who'd owned her must have had a sense of humor. And of course Frazzle was very close to Dazzle. It seemed like a good omen.

So we took Dazzle home. I was proud of Davy for choosing an older dog, and told him so. He replied, "Well, she looked at me like she already knew me. And I figured she might have a much harder time finding a home than one of those puppies."

"Good for you," I said. Then I asked him how he'd come up with the name Dazzle. He kind of grinned at me, and said, "It's not spelled the way you think, like it should be. I spell it D-A-Z-E-L."

"Okay," I said. "But how did you come up with that?"

Davy said, "Think of the letters, Grandpa. D-A-Z-E-L. I bet you can figure it out."

I started turning the letters around in my head. "Oh, my God," I said. "It's Zelda inside out!"

"I knew you'd get it," said my grandson.

—*Ray, 63*

Do Blondes Have More Fun?

*T*here's that old saying, "Life begins at forty," and I guess that's supposed to mean that by then your children are pretty much grown and you'll have more time for yourself. But in my case, I'd change that to "Life begins again at fifty-five," because that's how old I was when my daughter Laurie had her first child. She and her sweet husband Matt named the baby after me—Janet.

I was thrilled beyond words, for more than

the usual reasons. You see, I'd lost my husband Bob to a heart attack fourteen months earlier. I'd become quite the recluse. All our friends tried to pry me out of the house for lunch or shopping or a movie, or later for parties, but I wasn't having any of it. Their hearts were certainly in the right place, but I began to not pick up the phone, or even answer the door. I hate to say this, but my best "buddy" for a while was Sammy, the delivery boy for the liquor store. Not wise. Not wise at all. But enough of that. It's history.

Then Janet came into our lives—a healthy blond baby with Paul Newman–blue eyes. There was never a more beautiful little girl. I know all grandmothers say that, even if the baby looks like the offspring of a rhinoceros, but Janet really was special. And, yes, I spoiled her to death. Laurie finally put her foot down. "Mother, Matt and I can't afford to add a room to the house just to have a place to put all the presents you bring Janet. Get a grip." Well, I was crushed, but I got the message.

The years went by, and by the time Janet's younger sister Judy came along, Janet was already showing signs of being a real tomboy. She was five then, and was a terrific swimmer and always climbing trees. I soon discovered that when I did buy a present for Janet—and I tried to stick to special occasions—she was going to be happiest if it came from a sporting goods store. No dolls for Janet. Have you ever tried to giftwrap an adjustable basketball hoop on a stand? That's an adventure, I can tell you.

By the time she was sixteen, Janet was the star of her high school girls' basketball team. Judy was twelve, and as different as could be. She's pretty, too, but in a quieter way, with brown hair and hazel eyes. She'd decided she was going to be a movie star by then, with maybe an apprenticeship as head cheerleader along the way. Judy was just beginning to get a few hairs on her legs, but because she had dark hair, they were more obvious than the peach fuzz Janet had. In preparation for Hollywood stardom, Judy wanted to shave her legs. At twelve! Well, Laurie said that since she did have dark hair, she could begin shaving when Janet did, but of course Janet just didn't care.

So Judy hatched a plan. Janet sleeps like the proverbial brick—all that exercise. In the middle of the night, Judy crept into Janet's room with her mother's razor in hand and shaved Janet's legs. When Janet woke up in the morning, she started screaming about being attacked. Her legs had bled in several places where Judy had gotten careless in her haste. After calming Janet down and patching her up, Laurie turned her attention to Judy. My daughter is a very even-tempered woman, but not this morning. She told Judy that she would have to come straight home from school, and that she couldn't go to any friends' houses or have them over to her house, for two weeks. Judy kind of stared at her and said, "But I can start shaving my legs now, right?" Well, Laurie blew a gasket. "Don't you understand the English language? You're grounded, for two weeks! And no, you can't shave your legs until Janet does. And I mean Janet herself, while she's awake!"

Laurie told me all this in great detail, and I'm afraid I started laughing, and just couldn't stop. By the time she was through, Laurie was laughing, too. Oh, yes, and Janet began shaving her legs as soon as the scabs from Judy's botched job had healed. Pure self-defense, I'm sure.

But that's not the end of the story. It was May when all this happened, and we live in Daytona Beach, Florida, so the weather was already hot. While she was grounded, Judy was going out in the backyard and sunbathing. She asked her mother if she could put some lemon juice on her hair. This was a week into the grounding, and Laurie was beginning to feel a little sorry for her, and she knew how much Judy envied Janet's blond hair, so she said yes.

Judy was using more than lemon juice, however. She must have gotten hold of some dye from the drugstore, because suddenly she was alarmingly blond. Laurie decided to pretty much ignore it. She just said, "I had no idea lemon juice worked so well." Judy replied, "It's wonderful, isn't it?"

But then the two weeks were up, and one afternoon after school Judy went over to the house of a friend who had a pool. Her friend's father had mistakenly doubled the amount of the chlorine in the water, and all the girls suddenly found themselves with very red eyes. But Judy had a bigger problem. The chlorine reacted somehow with the hair dye she'd used and she came out of the pool with green hair. And I mean chartreuse! I happened to be at their house when she came home. She came in the kitchen door behind me and I saw Laurie's jaw drop. "My God," she said. "What have you done to yourself now?"

Now, when I was young this would be a very moral tale, about a young girl trying to fool Mother Nature and getting her comeuppance. But not these days. Judy's green hair was a huge hit at school. The principal wasn't amused, though, and called Laurie up pronto. Laurie explained that it was an accident, and told him all about the chlorine. The principal said he didn't care how it happened, Judy had to get rid of it. So Laurie dragged Judy off to the beauty parlor to try to get her normal hair color back. It seemed to work, but within a day the underlying green started to show again, just darker this time. It was almost the end of summer before enough new hair had grown in for the green to disappear entirely.

This all happened last year. We're keeping our fingers crossed for this year. Of course, Laurie and I understand, in a way. We're both brunettes, like Judy. Janet gets her blond hair from her dad. And brunettes always do have the suspicion that blondes have more fun. What makes it worse for poor Judy is that Janet couldn't care less what color her hair is, as long as her school wins the county basketball championship this year.

—*Janet, 68*

I'm Here, Too

$\mathcal{M}$y daughter's first marriage was a rocky one. Nobody was really at fault. Or, my daughter would create problems one day, my son-in-law the next. They married too young, I said so from the beginning, and they weren't as compatible as it seemed on the surface. They kept things going for fifteen years—quite a long time, considering the problems. I thought it was probably for the best when they finally got divorced, except for my grandson, Sammy. He was fourteen at the time, and at the age when you need all the parental support you can get. I'd always been close to Sammy, took him to his first NBA game, taught him to play golf, even went to country concerts with him. And I saw even more of him after his parents divorced. He'd come over and tell me his problems, and I'd try to give him some grand-fatherly advice.

Both his father and my daughter Janice got remarried within a year. Sammy's dad moved away, which meant Sammy only got to see him a couple of times a year. Janice's second marriage was to a man who owned the best restaurant here in town. He'd been mar-ried before, too, but he didn't have any chil-dren, and he really didn't know how to deal with Sammy. He didn't even know how to talk to him. It's not that Jack's a bad fellow. He treats Janice extremely well, and I'm grateful for that. And of course he's very busy. The restaurant business isn't easy, especially when it's a gourmet establishment like Jack's, where the customers expect a lot and let you know if they don't get it.

But Sammy was beginning to feel lonely. Jack was perfectly pleasant with him, and didn't give him a hard time. There was none of that "shape up or else" stuff a kid can get from a stepfather. Jack saved that for the employees at his restaurant, I guess, which I'm sure is necessary if you're going to maintain standards.

What bothered me most was that Sammy was getting whiny. He'd never been like that, despite the problems between his parents. I didn't like to see it happening. Every time we were together, he'd spend half the time complaining. One day he came over and started moaning about not having a car. He'd just turned sixteen and gotten his license. He was going on about how all his friends had cars—we've all heard that story one way or another. I told him to talk to Jack about it. His stepfather had all kinds of connections, so maybe he could come up with a jalopy for cheap. Sammy said, "I can't ask Jack for a car. You don't give cars to people who are just guests in your house." Well, that stopped me for a minute. I could see how Sammy felt more like a guest than a son, even a stepson.

So I told Sammy I'd lend him the money to buy an old car provided he got a job, after school, weekends, whatever, and paid me back part of what he earned each week. Here was Grandpa working out the kind of deal a father usually does. Sammy brightened up at that and said he'd look for a job.

Two weeks later I was over at Janice and Jack's

house for a Monday dinner—the day the restaurant was closed. There was another couple there, too, old friends of Jack's. Sammy was pretty quiet, as usual. But then he suddenly piped up and said that I'd agreed to lend him the money to buy a used car, and that he'd gotten a job to pay me back gradually. Jack kind of looked at me. All I could do was shrug. I thought it was a strange moment to bring all this up. But then I remembered that when she was a teenager, Janice had a habit of springing awkward news when there were guests around. Stops parents from blowing their stacks, that does. I must say I kind of grinned to myself.

Jack wanted to know what kind of job Sammy had found. Sammy smiled and said, "I'm going to be a busboy on weekends at Chez Armand." Dead silence around the table. Chez Armand was a new place that had just opened, and it was in direct competition with Jack's place. Well, I thought, that's one way to get noticed. After a long pause, Jack said, "That's interesting. We'll have to talk about that." I had to hand it to him—he was pretty calm.

The upshot was that Sammy went to work for Jack instead of Chez Armand. Sammy says Jack is a stickler about details, but that he's fair. And the two of them are finally getting to know each other. Jack bought Sammy a ten-year-old Chevy, so out of date it's becoming cool again, as Sammy puts it. And Sammy is repaying Jack out of his weekly wages. I look at it this way. I gave Sammy some good grandfatherly advice, Sammy gave his own creative twist to it, and I didn't even have to loan him any money. Not a bad deal. But the best thing about it is that Sammy isn't whining any more, and he's beginning to establish a genuine father/son relationship with Jack. He's also fun to be with again, the way a grandson should be.

—Mike, 67

The Wasp Sting

*M*y husband and I had a summer house on Long Island for a great many years. On the north shore, not the Hamptons, I hasten to say. It wasn't anything grand, but we had wonderful times there with the kids, and eventually with our grandchildren. There was a public beach on the Sound, open to residents only. Once, when our grandson Teddy was about five, he was charging up and down the beach, racing from the dunes straight down to the water at full tilt, laughing when he hit the water and caused it to splash all over the place. He'd done this about three times, but when he went back up to the dunes again we heard him wail suddenly. He came running down to us and was obviously in considerable pain. We gathered that he'd been stung, apparently by a wasp, because he said it was big and black. He was making quite a racket. I'd never seen him cry like that.

From a little way down the beach, a neighbor came trotting over to see what the matter was. He was a doctor, a rather famous one who headed the pediatric unit at a major New York hospital, but who was by then close to retirement. We had a perfectly cordial relationship with him, but we didn't really like him all that much. He was not a man who wore his eminence lightly. He grabbed Teddy's arm, a bit roughly I thought, and looked at it. "Don't be such a sissy," he said to Teddy, and told me and my husband to put some wet sand on the sting. I thanked him and he went off up the beach again. My husband Lew did not thank him, and said afterward, "I wouldn't let a man like that near me. How he got to be a famous children's doctor is beyond me."

We put the wet sand on Teddy's arm, and it seemed to work. He quieted down fairly quickly. There was a nasty welt around the sting for several days, and the episode rankled Lew for a long time. He has never been a fan of doctors, however. I pretty much put it out of mind, but then years later something happened that brought it all back.

Teddy was fourteen by then, a very bright and very nice boy, indeed. He and our granddaughter Tally were out visiting on Long Island again, with their parents due on the weekend. I'd gone to the supermarket with Tally, and when we got home, Teddy came out to help us carry the grocery bags into the house. Teddy picked up one paper bag that was fairly light by putting his thumb on the outside and his forefinger on the inside. Then he let out a yelp and dropped it. He'd been stung again, right in the fleshy part between the two fingers. But after the first surprise he picked up the bag again and carried it into the house, along with another one. About five minutes later, he sat down at the kitchen table and said, "I can't breathe very well, Grandma." I looked at him, and he was very flushed. His sister Tally was only eleven, but she turned around and looked at him and said, "Grandma, call 911."

I said, "What?"

"Call 911, *right away*. I'm going to get my asthma inhaler." And she rushed out of the kitchen.

I was stunned for a moment. She had used a voice a grandparent is more likely to use on a child than the other way around. But another glance at Teddy told me she was right. He looked dreadful, and his breathing was getting quite labored.

I called 911, and the operator was wonderful. I quickly explained the problem, and she asked if we had any antihistamines. I told her my granddaughter had asthma and was getting her inhaler. She said good, and that an ambulance would be there in five minutes. By the time I hung up, Teddy was using Tally's inhaler. By then I was quite frightened.

The ambulance came screaming up to the house, and the paramedic immediately gave Teddy an injection. Then they helped him out to the ambulance. I went with them. Teddy was lying in the back breathing heavily, and his face and arms and legs were covered with huge red welts. But the injection was taking hold and at least his breathing was better. They kept him overnight at the county hospital, but even when he came home he had to stay in bed for another three days. His entire body was covered with those welts, and he was quite shaky.

He recovered completely, of course, but from then on he had to keep antihistamines with him at all times during the warm months. Allergies to bee stings, I learned, can be fatal. We were lucky that Tally had her inhaler, and that she realized what the problem was, much better than Teddy or I did. Lew had been out playing golf, but when he got back and heard what had happened, he said, "I knew it, I knew there was a reason Teddy howled so much when he got stung on the beach that time and that damned pediatrician called him a sissy. Teddy's body was telling him even then, 'This is serious, kid.' " I've learned since that some people can be stung several times without much effect, and then go into toxic shock—which was what had happened to Teddy when he couldn't breathe—on the tenth sting. It had only taken two stings to get Teddy to that point, and with some people it takes only one. The world, you realize sometimes, can be very dangerous to some people in ways that affect other people hardly at all.

At the end of that summer we ended up at a party that was also attended by the famous pediatrician. Well, Lew went after him. He asked if he remembered the first bee sting when Teddy was five. Not surprisingly, the doctor had no recollection of it. "Well," said Lew, "you called my grandson a sissy. This summer he got stung for the second time in his life and nearly died, you old fool." There was dead

111

silence around us, and I thought I would dearly love to be somewhere else. But the pediatrician, who was now in his seventies, just clapped Lew on the shoulder and said, "Good for you, Lew. What use are grandfathers if they can't defend a grandson's honor?" Even Lew smiled, and I thought to myself that I had an idea why the pediatrician had been such a success.

—*Liz, 68*

The Girl from Belgrade

*W*ho can figure kids out? I've been trying to do it for a lifetime, but there are times when I'm still baffled. Kids are fascinating creatures—good ones, bad ones, they can be equally mysterious. Now, of course there are people who think they know what makes kids tick, experts of all kinds who claim to have the whole thing down pat. They can throw statistics at you, and present very impressive "developmental theories," or come to very specific conclusions based on their long experience. But you'll notice that all these psychologists and social relations experts—not to mention school principals and guidance counselors— keep coming up with different answers and getting into nasty arguments about who's right.

The problem is that the experts are always trying to shove kids into pigeonholes, which the kids themselves do their very best to climb right back out of. I don't believe in pigeonholes. It seems to me that every human being on the planet is unique, and that we'd all understand one another a lot better if we'd accept that as a starting point.

I grew up in a family with a lot of kids. I had two older brothers, a younger sister, and a baby brother. We were very evenly spaced—one of us came along every two years. Then there were two cousins who stayed with us every summer. Their parents were actors, and they usually did touring shows in the summer, playing a week or two at eight or nine different theaters. So every June, July, and August, our house became what my mother called "Camp Chaos." We had a wonderful time, whether we were laughing or quarreling. A wonderful time quarreling, you ask? Is this old lady crazy? Not at all. Shared laughter is very joyous and unifying, but when there are seven kids involved, and a quarrel starts between two of them, the other five end up taking sides, and you can learn a great deal about yourself that way. People who grew up in small families never understand this, but people from large families invariably do.

Large families often end up producing a teacher or two, and so it was with me, my oldest brother, and one of my cousins. I went away to college at seventeen with the intention of becoming the world's greatest teacher. I started off teaching first grade and ended up teaching high school seniors. Along the way, I got to see how kids behave at every age. I retired when I was sixty-five, and was bored in about two weeks. My daughter Patricia had predicted that. I had only two children, Patricia and Warren. I would have liked more, but that wasn't to be. Warren is in the foreign service and he and his family have lived all over the globe. But Patricia and her family—her husband Grant and my two grandsons, Randy and Scott—live just a few blocks away from me.

Patricia didn't just warn me that I'd be bored when I retired; she also had a possible solution. She urged me to offer myself as a tutor, helping individual students with problem subjects in the late afternoons and some evenings. With so many parents frantic about their kids' educational future these days, I've had no shortage of pupils. I taught most of their parents in school over the years, so they know and trust me, if I do say so myself. But I've also had some pupils whose families moved here from other places, and who heard about me from neighbors or friends. That's how I got one of my most interesting students, whom I call the girl from Belgrade.

Her name was Gina. Her parents were both teachers in Belgrade, and they saw the trouble that was coming, which would lead to the NATO bombing in early 1999. They felt it was their duty to stay, and hoped to be able to help eventually in putting their country back together. But they were against the policies of the government, and were afraid for the safety of their daughter. So they sent her to America to live with an older aunt and uncle here where I live in Maryland. The aunt and uncle had no children of their own, and even though they had been in the United States since the early 1980s and had become citizens, there was a lot about America they didn't fully understand, especially when it came to kids. They welcomed Gina warmly, and were very good to her, but they couldn't really connect to some of her problems.

Gina was supposedly sent to me to be tutored in English, something she really didn't need. Both of her parents spoke English, as so many intellectuals in Europe do, and aside from her accent, she didn't really need my help much with the language. But she did need help in other ways. Gina missed her parents, of course, but she was also having trouble fitting in at high school. She was quite pretty, but she was somewhat shy by nature so that being a stranger in a strange land, she found it difficult to make friends. She dressed a little too formally, and wore no makeup except for lipstick, while most of the other girls had on enough mascara to join a rock band. She also liked classical music and jazz, which wasn't exactly the taste of her classmates.

Gina came to see me twice a week, and we'd do a little work, mostly a matter of correcting her pronunciation. But what she really needed was someone to talk to. I also started collecting cartoons and jokes to go over with her—quite naturally, she simply didn't "get" a lot of American humor. Ancient as I am, forty-five years of teaching kids has kept me very aware of the changing form of adolescent humor, enough so that I would occasionally make Gina blush. Although I swear very little myself, I am not afraid of "dirty" words, and I think that being able to talk about some of the things that puzzled her with a gray-haired widow was quite reassuring.

But I felt that something more was needed, and I decided to enlist the help of my grandson Randy. Randy is a very popular, funny, and good-looking young man, but he's never been able to fool me. Underneath his surface breeziness—which is very useful in a social way—he's quite a serious person. So one day, I asked him if he knew anything about Gina. It turned out that he knew who she was, but not much more. They were both seniors, but it's a big school, over 1,700 students, and they weren't taking any classes together. Randy said that some of his friends had said that she acted "superior" to everyone. I suggested that that was because she was shy and perhaps even a little frightened. Randy nodded and said, "Could be."

I asked Randy if he'd be willing to drop by one evening when I was scheduled to see Gina, and try to get to know her a little. Randy rolled his eyes, and then grinned and said, "For you, Grandma, anything." He showed up a few nights later and played his part to perfection. He handed me a manila envelope and said, "Mom asked me to drop this by, Grandma. Sorry to interrupt." He smiled at Gina and I introduced them properly and asked if he wanted to join us in a soda and some cookies. "Sure, why not?" said my well-trained grandson.

Randy can draw anybody out in conversation. He actually reads the newspaper—something he doesn't necessarily emphasize with some of his friends—and is surprisingly well informed. And he has the gift of gab, something that runs in my family. Gina was a bit stiff at first, but I could see her relaxing, and before long he actually had her laughing. Nobody can resist Randy for long. When he was a little younger, I worried he might grow up to be a politician, but he's a little too genuine for that. And he's not quite sufficiently stuck on himself. He's really interested in other people.

Over the next few weeks, Randy dropped in again from time to time, always with a good excuse, so Gina wouldn't get suspicious. And he started talking to her at school, just casually in the halls or wherever. He also saw to it that she got to know his friend Vivian a little. Viv, as everyone calls her, and Randy have been pals since the second grade. It's the kind of friendship where they will both start laughing at the same time and no one has the faintest idea what's so funny. There was a time when I used to try to get them to explain what they were laughing about, but Randy would say, "Life, Grandma, life." Viv would howl with laughter and Randy would look terribly serious and then she'd try to look serious as well, and he'd start laughing. Fascinating, as I said at the beginning. And totally mysterious. I gave up, of course, trying to understand. Instead I'd just stare at them as though they were from Mars. They liked that, and would laugh even harder. I enjoyed being part of their game that way, even though I didn't have a clue what the rules really were.

Viv is an important part of this story. All during her senior year, she had been dating a young man who was a sophomore in college. They were quite serious about each other. Randy wasn't dating anyone in particular. His girlfriend, Diana, had moved to California with her family the previous summer, and they were still mooning over each other via E-mail. The senior prom was coming up in May, and there's a rule that you can't bring a date who isn't enrolled at the school. Idiotic, I think, but the kind of thing people get to be principals by thinking up. And with Diana in California, it had been agreed that Randy and Viv would go together. But it turned out, quite naturally, that Gina had not been asked to the prom.

Now, Randy wasn't interested in Gina romantically. Diana was still very much in the picture and they were plotting to go to the same college. But Gina had blossomed a good deal with Randy's help, and he was fond of her. He also thought that it wasn't right that a nice girl from a foreign country, whose parents were in some danger back in her homeland, should be left out of the senior prom. He said to me, "You know, Grandma, it just isn't hospitable." I agreed with him entirely. Randy said he'd been thinking of asking Viv if she'd be really upset if he took Gina to the prom. He wanted my opinion as to whether he ought to try to arrange things that way. Stupidly, I said I was sure Viv would understand. After all, she had a serious boyfriend and she could always arrange to do something with him that night. I started this story by wondering who could really understand kids, including me, even though I've spent a lifetime teaching them. But of course given the opportunity to open my mouth, I stuck my foot right in it.

Viv was furious! She had a tantrum that Randy described as something out of a disaster movie, with whole villages being buried under lava from a volcano. "Now I know how they must have felt at Pompeii," he told me. "She says she'll never speak to me again, Grandma!" And to make matters worse, he'd asked Gina *before* telling Viv about the idea. I asked him why in the world he'd done that. "Because Gina might have said no. I mean, she knew I was planning to go with Viv, and I thought maybe . . . oh, never mind." I said, "You thought maybe you could get credit for asking Gina without having to even bring it up with Viv. Right?"

Randy said. "That's nasty, Grandma," and stalked out of the house.

Well! Viv was a volcano, Randy felt buried under her lava and scorched by my judgment, and I felt like a fool. And of course very guilty and sad. I'd offended my beloved grandson. The only one who was happy was Gina, who had no idea of the trouble she'd caused. I thanked my lucky stars she wasn't scheduled to come over that night. I was in a state, and probably would have snapped at her, even though she was completely innocent.

It was my meddling that had created this whole mess. Grandma didn't sleep very well that night, I can tell you. And that's never been a problem of mine.

This all happened on a Saturday. Late Sunday afternoon, Viv called Randy and apologized for blowing her stack. Randy apologized for having invited Gina without telling Viv first. I called Randy to apologize for being a meddling old lady. Randy said, "No, Grandma, what you said was true, I just didn't want to admit it." A half hour later my daughter called to find out what in the world was going on. I said, "Life, Patricia, life," and started laughing. My daughter said, "Mother, that's Randy's line!" I told her I was aware of that and started laughing again. Patricia said, "I give up," and started laughing, too.

Randy and Gina went to the prom together. Viv even went with Gina to help her pick out a dress. She told me later that it had been hard to explain that while what Gina usually wore to school wasn't sufficiently grungy, when it came to proms all the girls wanted to look like their mothers did twenty-five years ago but with more cleavage showing. Viv and her boyfriend went to a Baltimore Orioles game on prom night, and the Orioles actually won, something they weren't prone to do that year.

I stayed home and watched a very peculiar foreign film with subtitles on BRAVO. It made as much sense to me as anything else, and even appeared to have a happy ending.

—*Martha, 71*

Daily Communication

$\mathscr{I}$ was a schoolteacher, and my husband Harold was an editor at our local newspaper. Harold was ten years older than I was, and we both retired at the same time in 1990, when he was sixty-five and I was fifty-five. We were both somewhat relieved to escape the great surge of computer use that took place in the 1990s. Harold had to learn to use one at work, but he didn't like it much. He admitted that it speeded some things up, and made sense economically, but he also felt that reporters were getting much sloppier. They'd just move a paragraph around on the computer without bothering to take the trouble to rewrite the end of the previous paragraph properly, so that the text would flow easily. And reporters were making more mistakes, too. Not spelling errors so much, the computer usually took care of that. But somebody would be identified as a Mr. in one paragraph and as Ms. two paragraphs later, that kind of thing. He'd say, jokingly, "I know gender doesn't mean what it once did in our society, and a good thing, too, but this is ridiculous. You can't have people changing sex from one paragraph to the next."

I'd escaped computers altogether, just barely. I wasn't against them in principle, though I do think children ought to be able to do basic math in their heads, and a lot of them can't anymore. You produce the extra two pennies at the store, and the teenager making change practically has a nervous breakdown.

This kind of complaint is looked upon as fuddy-duddyism in many quarters, of course. I was always willing to recognize that computers were the shape of the future, but I kept wondering what would happen in a real catastrophe down the line. It seemed to me we were putting all our eggs into one technological basket, so to speak.

But both Harold and I tended to keep our mouths shut about this kind of thing when we went to visit our daughter and her husband in California. The companies they worked for were computerized to the hilt, and they had a PC at home as well. Our grandchildren, Jeff and Mariah, started playing computer games at an age when I'd been excited by hopscotch and Harold was building forts with Lincoln Logs. The world moves on, and we were glad for Jeff and Mariah that they'd been born into the start of a new age. We understood that it would be extremely exciting for them.

Harold and I had eight lovely years of retirement together, traveling a good deal and generally doing as we pleased. Then Harold died very suddenly of a massive heart attack. My daughter tried to persuade me to move out to California, but that would have meant leaving behind many good friends and the pleasure of running into former students all over town. One of the great satisfactions of teaching is the affection with which a former little rascal greets you when he's thirty. It's very sustaining, and I didn't want to lose that connection with the past.

It took about a year for my daughter to

come to terms with the fact that I was staying put where I was. When she did, she started trying to persuade me that I should get a computer, and start using the Internet to communicate with her and the kids. "Oh, Barbara," I said, "you know me and technology. It took me four years to learn to program the VCR. Computers really aren't for me." Barbara said that was nonsense. They were going to buy me one of the new iMacs, and Jeff was going to come East for the month of July and teach me how to use it.

I didn't know what to say. Jeff had just turned twelve, and even though I knew he was a whiz with computers, I wondered if he could really teach someone like me to use one. But I could hardly say no to a month-long visit from my grandson. Harold and I had flown out to California every year since our retirement, and I'd seen Jeff grow from a kindergarten tyke to the verge of adolescence. I was extremely fond of him, and of his sister, who was two years younger. So I talked to Jeff about the idea on the telephone. I told him I was willing to try, but that he'd have to be very patient with me, since I could be quite stupid about mechanical things. Of course "mechanical" was the wrong word, and he corrected me, but very sweetly. I said, "Okay, let's try it." But I must say I was quite anxious about it. I hardly slept at all the night before he arrived on July 2nd.

I drove out to the airport to get him, and of course he'd grown several inches since I'd seen him the year before. It was the first trip he'd made alone on a plane, and he was quite excited about that, telling me all kinds of funny stories about the other passengers. I was just delighted to see him, and I thought, "This is going to be fun, even if I'm a flop at the computer." The iMac had already arrived, but was still sitting there in its cartons. I hadn't dared unpack it by myself. He said we'd set it up the next day. I'm sure he would have liked to do it right away, but I guess Barbara had warned him not to push me.

The next morning he got everything hooked up for me, explaining very carefully what he was doing as he went along. I kept nodding, and a couple of times I asked a question, but that was mostly just to seem as though I was paying attention. My mind wasn't really absorbing what he was doing. But it didn't seem quite as complicated as I'd expected. I'd read many times that the computers from Apple were easier to use, and I could tell that was probably true, simply because I wasn't feeling panicky about what was going on.

So there was this new futuristic machine sitting in the study, looking very handsome, I had to admit. I'd asked for a purple model. Purple is my favorite color. Silly as it may seem, I felt that a purple computer was much friendlier than if it had been plain gray. Jeff said, "Okay, Grandma, let's send an E-mail to Mariah. She'll be wondering why I'm taking so long."

So he typed up a message that began, "Greetings from Grandma's house." And in what seemed like no time at all, we had a message back that began, "What took you so long, Big Brother?" Jeff rolled his eyes at that, of course, and said, "See."

I patted Jeff on the shoulder and said, "Tell Mariah Grandma says she's very impressed with Big Brother."

"Thank you, Grandma," Jeff said. "It's fun, isn't it?"

"Yes," I said. "It is fun, but that's because you're doing it."

"Don't worry, Grandma, you'll get the hang of it in no time."

Well, it wasn't no time, but I did get the hang of it. He was really amazingly patient with me. He didn't get annoyed with me once, although I gave him plenty of cause. It was a real lesson in role reversal, I can tell you. I'd spent thirty years teaching kids just Jeff's age, but in this situation I was very much the pupil, and he was very much the teacher in ways that seemed beyond his years. I talked to Barbara about it later, and she said that there was something interesting going on with kids and computers when they were with much older people. "Ahem," I said, and Barbara laughed. "You know what I mean, Mother. But I think smart kids like Jeff understand instinctively with older people that they are communicating with a different space-time continuum in a way. It's almost as though they've come back from the future in a time machine, and they can be amazingly adult all of a sudden. Jeff is not always so grown-up, I assure you."

I understood what she meant. Although he gave me a lesson every day, we did a lot of other things during the month he was with me. And when we went to see the fireworks on the Fourth, or drove to the beach, or took in a movie, he acted like any other twelve-year-old. Then, he'd be full of excitement, with sudden rushes of emotion and even the occasional moment of rebellion. But when we were in front of the computer, and he was teaching me, he was serious in a way that was worthy of someone ten years older.

By the time he went back to California at the end of the month, I was getting fairly comfortable with what I was doing at the computer. But when the first E-mail came in from California, saying, "Jeff here, reporting safe return," I felt a moment of anxiety. Was I really going to be able to do this all by myself? I took a deep breath to calm myself down. Then I typed out the following words: "Grandma at the controls on her first solo flight. Does control tower read me?"

Jeff replied, "Control tower reads smart Grandmother loud and clear."

Since then, I've been in almost daily communication with my grandchildren, and feeling extremely up to date.

—*Nora, 65*

6

returning the favor

Grandparents do a great many different things for their grandchildren. If they live close by, they may take a very active part in nurturing a child. Visits to or from grandparents who live far away become special events in the life of a child, highly anticipated and filled with warm memories. A grandparent may play a great many different roles as the child grows up: teacher, travel guide, confidante, mediator between child and parent, or simple cheerleader. Grandparents are repositories of knowledge and dispensers of wisdom, someone to laugh with or, sometimes, the best lap in the world to cry in. They are usually mentors, and often become the dearest of friends.

In return, grandparents derive enormous pleasure from their relationship with a grandchild. Grandchildren are a reward in themselves, but sometimes, as the child grows older, he or she becomes something more. Few things in life are more rewarding than when a grandchild unexpectedly returns the favor of a grandparent's love and does something to lift a grandparent's spirits by solving a problem or simply springing a wonderful surprise.

In this chapter a grandmother tells how two grandsons helped to put a lifetime of memories in order, and a grandfather tells how his stepgrandson became a fresh pair of eyes. A granddaughter finds a way to restore a lost treasure, and

127

a whole family of grandchildren collaborate on the creation of a grand surprise. A woman who just can't seem to give up smoking is cured of the habit by a very clever granddaughter. And a grandmother who has suffered a stroke discovers the full meaning of the word "devotion."

All these grandparents are the beneficiaries of the love they have given their grandchildren, as it is returned to them in the fullest measure.

Memory Lane Is More Than It Used to Be

Unlike my sister, who has never thrown anything away in her entire life, I am not a pack rat—sorry, "collector." When something breaks in my house it goes into the garbage. For old clothing, of course, I call up the Salvation Army or the Junior League thrift shop. Or, I call my sister. I remember alerting her that I had found a 1960 television set with a broken screen in my basement. She was over in a flash, took it home, gutted the whole thing and turned it into a planter on her terrace. Ugliest thing you have ever seen. But whatever makes you happy, right?

The one thing I will not part with is all the old photographs of my family. Photos that go back to the "Ice Age," as my daughter Jane puts it. My great-grandmother Emily started this when she got married at seventeen. From then on, the pictures were handed down from generation to generation. About twice a year

128

I'd go up to the attic, where they are stored in two big boxes, and drag them down to look at. It's always made me happy. Jane didn't like the fact that those boxes were up in the attic. She'd say, "If the house ever catches on fire, you'll get yourself killed trying to save them. And I worry about you going up to the attic by yourself, anyway. At your age, Mama, broken hips are all the rage." Bless her heart, I know she has my best interests in mind, but I do get tired of all the suggestions that I'm as old as the hills. I'm only seventy-two, for heaven's sake!

Unfortunately, Jane never really cared about the photos. I love my only daughter very much, but she's of that generation that turned its back on the past. Television did that. Jane's attitude made me worry about what would happen to the pictures after I'm gone. I made her promise to give them to the local historical society if she doesn't want them, but I doubt if they'd be all that interested, either. My family wasn't quite prominent enough.

But then I got a surprise. One afternoon last winter, I was in the mood to go through the pictures, and went up to the attic and carried them down to the dining room table. Two trips that takes, these days. I do try to be careful. I was sitting there going through them and my grandson Carl came bounding into the house. He's Jane's oldest, fourteen now. Carl often pops in for a visit. What a fine boy he is. He usually stays for about half an hour, but that day he stayed for two hours while I went through the pictures with him. You could have knocked me over with a feather. He was fascinated. He wants to direct movies someday, so maybe that's what caught his interest—looking at the past, seeing how things were. We had a wonderful time, and I got a bit teary after he left, thinking maybe the photos would have a place in the family after all.

About six weeks later, during Easter vacation, I flew to California to visit my son Steve and his family. I always look forward to that. Steve always records my visits on video, but he's not interested in my old pictures, either. I stayed for a week, but it felt like three days to me. But you know what they say about houseguests—after a week they begin to smell like fish. I'm afraid that's true. My other sister, Bea, visited me last year for a week that turned into three. By the end of ten days I was ready to shoot her, although of course I tried not to show it. She'd just lost her husband—my Bob died eight years ago—so she needed company.

When I got back, Jane and the kids came to get me at the airport. They always roll out the welcome mat when I get back from a trip. It makes me feel very lucky. And neither of Jane's boys had ever given me that "What did you bring me?" stuff. I have to hand it to Jane on that. They do have manners. Of course, I always do bring them some little something, but they know they won't get it for a day or two, until I get unpacked.

Anyway, they drove me home, and we all went in for cookies and Diet Pepsi, as we always do. As we went through the dining room, I noticed this big package on the table, beautifully wrapped. "Now, what in the world is that?" I asked. Carl piped up and said it was for me but I couldn't open it until they'd left. So we had our Oreos and Pecan Sandies, and I told them more about their Uncle Steve and Aunt Lois and their cousins. But as we all munched away, I kept wondering what was in the package. Finally Jane said I looked tired and they should get out of there and let me have a nap.

Well, the minute the front door closed, I sprinted back to the dining room to open my package. Such beautiful gold wrapping paper! Jane's doing, no doubt. Too bad it was going to be torn to shreds in about ten seconds. If it were my sister Annie, it would have been unwrapped with the greatest of care, and the paper would have been recycled. She has an incredible memory about that, I must say. You never get your own wrapping paper back.

So I tore the paper off and opened the box, and there were ten photograph albums—the kind with slightly sticky pages and clear plastic over them, so the photos don't get spoiled with glue. And there were all my photos from the boxes in the attic, in perfect order. And Carl had used his computer to type out all the captions from the back of the photos and put the information under each one. It must have taken him days of work.

They're very handsome albums, and they look just splendid in my living room. Jane told me later that she'd paid for the albums. "I thought it was a worthwhile investment to keep you out of that damn attic," she said. But the whole thing had been Carl's idea, and he'd done all the work with help from his younger brother Ken. Jane was amazed because Ken, who's ten, actually took instructions from his older brother while they were doing it. I could tell Jane was quite proud of them. As for me, I was touched beyond anything I can put into words. I understand all about generation gaps, but in this case Carl and Ken took a running leap and sailed right over that particular chasm. Now, when I look at my great grandmother's wedding pictures, I think of my grandsons. It's all one continuous line in my head.

—*Abigail, 72*

A Fresh Pair of Eyes

*F*or forty years I taught high school English. I guess I did a decent enough job—even won a few awards. Forty years is a long time, but for me it seems like ten. I loved teaching and I loved all those kids, even the rotten apples. There are always a few in the barrel, but once in a while you can get through to one, and that's very rewarding. For some kids, though, the idea of reading a book, an entire book, is just horrifying. Their eyes glaze over at the thought of it. Television has made that problem worse, of course, but it was always there.

I'll never forget a boy named Bill Crow. This was fifteen years ago. The whole class was supposed to read Emily Brontë's *Wuthering Heights*. It's a great literary novel, of course, but it has a story that teenagers can get involved in. The boys often identify with Heathcliff—they tend to feel like outcasts themselves. And the girls like the romance. The ghostly aspects don't hurt, either. At any rate, the class was supposed to write a paper on the book. To my astonishment, Bill Crow, who was usually late, turned in his paper a couple of days early. I couldn't wait to get home and read it. Was it possible I was finally getting through to young Bill?

Well, the answer was no. His report wasn't bad, but it had a slight problem. It only covered half the novel. And he spelled Cathy's name "Kathi." I remembered that the famous black-and-white movie with Laurence Olivier and Merle Oberon had been on AMC over the previous weekend. That's a fine film, but of course it stops halfway through and doesn't tell the story of the next generation. I roared with laughter and so did my wife Marie. She said, "Well, that's a step up from reading Cliff Notes, at least." I had to agree with her, and so I didn't give Bill Crow an F. He got a C for calculating. I wrote a note at the top of the paper: "Keep trying, Bill. The beautiful Merle Oberon has always been one of my favorites, especially as *Cathy*." I heard recently that Bill is a lawyer in San Antonio now. He must have decided to do some work somewhere along the line.

This story may seem beside the point, but it isn't, as you'll see. I retired two years ago. Marie had passed away the year before, and I was at low ebb. Then I started having trouble with my eyes. I won't bore you with the medical details, but I've had laser treatments and take all kinds of drops, and nothing has helped much. Things have gotten progressively fuzzier, which is very hard for someone who's spent his life reading. I couldn't drive anymore, of course, which meant that my daughter and son-in-law had to take up the slack. But this came at a bad time for them, because Lizzie was having her first baby. It's a second marriage for both of them. Lizzie and her first husband didn't have any children, but Gene, her second husband, did. He has a son named Darryl, who lives with them. And here's why I told you about Bill Crow. The second or third time I saw Darryl—he was fifteen then—he told me he'd watched that 1939 version of *Wuthering Heights*. I asked him what he thought of it, and said he thought it was very good, but it was too bad they hadn't told the whole story. Well, I knew right then that Darryl and I were going to be good friends.

But more than that, Darryl's been my salvation. The first Christmas after Lizzie married Gene, Darryl gave me a subscription to the weekly large-print *New York Times*. *That* I could read. And it was entirely his idea. Then, when he turned sixteen, he got his license, and took over the chore of driving me around town. But that's only part of it. He goes to the library and picks out large-print books he thinks I might be interested in. And things that aren't available in large print, he reads aloud to me. He's been reading me a collection of great American short stories recently. Some of them are old favorites of mine, but he's encountering some of them for the first time. We talk about them afterward. He's very bright indeed, and I like to think that he's getting some return on his efforts, listening to me hold forth.

When Lizzie and Gene were first married, I used to introduce Darryl as my stepgrandson. That was stupid of me, and I soon changed it. I simply say he's my grandson. His father's parents died a number of years ago, and he doesn't have a relationship with his real mother's parents. He calls me "Grandpop." And to me, he's every inch a grandson. No man could ask for a better one.

—*Arthur, 67*

"House and Garden"

My late husband Thomas was a truly wonderful man, and we had forty-six lovely years together. But he did have one little flaw—everything had to be done his way. We had many a tiff over ridiculous things, and sometimes I got my way, when Thomas would decide that my way was actually his way after all. I wouldn't trade a minute of our life together, including the tiffs. We had two lovely daughters, and five terrific grandchildren, two from Peggy and three from Anne.

We spent the last thirty-five years in the same home—we'd moved twice before that. And through all that time both the inside and outside of the house were white, repainted every three years. Thomas didn't like wallpaper and he didn't like colored paint on the walls. I could put up all the pictures and mirrors I liked, so that gave the place some character, but the walls had to be white. What I wouldn't have given to have some wallpaper in the bedroom, and especially a kitchen with some color to it. I wanted a yellow kitchen, but Thomas just wouldn't have it, and eventually I gave up.

I think Thomas's aversion to color on the walls was due in part to the fact that he was allergic to almost any kind of flower you could grow. To him color meant sneezes. The allergies meant that we couldn't have a garden, either, just green lawn and a few evergreen shrubs. It got so that I forgot green was a color. It was the outside equivalent of white inside. Luckily, there were a couple of maple trees in the yard, and I loved fall, with all those lovely red and gold leaves.

Of course, when Thomas died two years ago, I didn't think, "Now I can have a yellow kitchen," or "Now I can have a garden." I just missed him dreadfully. I hardly knew what to do with myself. But four months after he died, my oldest and best friend Dot, who was also a widow, came charging into the house one day and said, "Mourning time is over, Cupcake." That's what she always called me, because I loved cupcakes so much when

I was a girl. That's what my grandchildren call me, too, although Thomas always called me Marie. Anyway, Dot came charging in and said, "We're going to Europe. Pack your bags."

Well, of course I hemmed and hawed, but Dot has always been very persuasive. I talked it over with my daughters and they urged me to go, too. And so did my grandchildren, who were all in high school or college by then. "Aunt Dot's got the right idea," they said. "Pack your bags, Cupcake."

Thomas and I had been to England a couple of times and to Rome once, but this was going to be a grand tour, two whole months. Dot's one of those people who's been everywhere, and she picks up languages, at least enough to get around, at the drop of a hat. So I knew I was in good hands. And, really, they speak English almost everywhere now, at least in the hotels and restaurants.

I won't bother you with travel tales. Let's just say I had a wonderful time everywhere we went, which was nine cities in five countries. I gained about ten pounds, most of it in Vienna, where I simply couldn't resist the pastries. Dot took to calling me Linzer Torte for a while. But two months is a long time, and I missed my daughters and their families. I'm lucky that they both live within half an hour of me, and I've had the privilege of watching my grandchildren grow up. I've always been very close to them, and they loved Thomas, too. So, as good a time as I had, I was more than ready to go home. I'd picked up presents for everyone along the way. Leather boxes for my grandsons in Florence, and beautiful scarves for my granddaughters in Paris, and gourmet goodies for my daughters and their husbands here and there along the way.

My daughter Peggy had driven Dot and me to the airport when we left, and Anne had said she'd meet us when we got back. But instead of Anne, there were all five grandchildren. What a greeting! It was early September when we got back, and the two oldest hadn't left for college yet. They'd all had summer jobs of one kind or another, close to home, so they were outdoing one another in telling funny stories about their experiences on the drive back in from the airport. Somehow, we'd managed to cram into the van, luggage and all. Dot lives closer to the airport than I do, so I thought they'd drop her off first, but they said one of the roads into town was under repair and took the long way around to avoid traffic, arriving at my house first. To my surprise, the kids suggested that Dot come in for a few minutes, they'd laid in some supplies and we'd have a snack. I should have known something was up, but I didn't.

The house was its old familiar white self, and I was very glad to see it. I had a momentary pang, remembering that Thomas wouldn't be there, but told myself to get a grip, as the kids say. So we all trooped in, and the minute we got into the front hall, I knew something was up. I smelled fresh paint.

I looked around at my grandchildren and they were all grinning like the Cheshire Cat. David and Leslie—they belong to Peggy—and

Jenny, Laura, and Chuck—they're Anne's—all had that kind of glow kids get when they're very excited. "What have you been up to around here?" I asked.

So they showed me. First the living room, which was Wedgewood blue with white trim, just like I'd always wanted, and then upstairs to the bedroom, which had the most glorious floral wallpaper and looked like a field in spring. And then back down to the kitchen, which was a lovely sunny yellow, again just what I'd always wanted. And as I was "ooh"ing in the kitchen I happened to look out the back window. I almost fainted dead away. There, along both sides of the yard, were twenty-foot-long flower beds, just bursting with late summer and early fall flowers.

David, who was twenty then, and six-foot-four, opened the back door and bowed me through it into the yard. It was all so beautiful I wanted to cry, so I did. I hugged all my grand-kids with the tears streaming down my cheeks, saying, "Thank you, thank you," over and over again. David and Jenny and Laura had done all the painting, it turned out, and Leslie and Chuck had done most of the work in the garden, but they'd all had a hand in picking out the flowers. And Dot said, "Oh, by the way, Cupcake, when we were in Holland I ordered some tulip and daffodil bulbs. They'll be arriving in two or three weeks for fall planting." She'd known what was going on the whole time! And Chuck said he'd put them in the ground when the time came. Chuck's the youngest, only four-teen then, but he'd always had a green thumb.

Well, I was just back from visiting great cities all over Europe, but I have to say that the grandest tour I've ever had was seeing the wonderful things my grandchildren had done right in my own house and backyard.
—*Marie ("Cupcake"), 69*

Home Nursing

*W*hen I was younger, I did all the right things health-wise. I had yearly check-up. Cut down on cholesterol and salt. I even took up jogging, and went for a swim every day when the weather was warm enough. I live on Long Island, and there's a beach just ten minutes away. All my friends marveled at my stamina, not to mention my trim figure. I was obviously invincible. Ha!

Then one morning two years ago I was jogging—in my brand-new, terribly spiffy pink jogging suit—when my right leg became numb, and then my right arm. And then I was flat on my back and couldn't even speak, let alone cry out for help. The next thing I knew, I was in the hospital with a nurse bending over me, and all these dreadful tubes and wires attached to my body. I could see and hear but not talk. Horrors! Nobody likes to talk more than I do. My first husband, who was the strong silent type, said that I was the perfect wife for him, because I talked enough for both of us. He was a darling. After he passed on, I married again, but that didn't work out. Herb said my talking drove him crazy, but what really bothered him was that I wouldn't give him control of my money, and I had a lot from my first husband. When Herb walked out, I took up the slack by talking to myself. I and I got along famously.

Well, I was lying there in the hospital unable to talk and full of tubes and thinking I'd just as soon be dead. I kept drifting in and out of sleep. I was full of drugs, of course, but hospitals are so noisy, and the minute you drift off, they wake you up to do something awful to you. But after I'd been there two days, I was awakened by a familiar voice saying, "All right, Grammy, enough of these cheap theatrics. Nice try, but it didn't work. Sorry."

It was my granddaughter Martha. I started crying the moment I realized who it was. In a very dramatic voice, Martha said, "I came as soon as I heard." And that made me want to laugh, although I couldn't manage much more than a gurgle. How many times had I heard that corny line in old black-and-white movies? Martha always spent part of the summer with me when she was growing up, and we used to watch old movies together and have a wonderful time. It was June when I had my stroke, and Martha's parents were in Europe, as usual. She was supposed to join them later, but that wasn't to be. Martha said I'd be in the hospital for another two weeks and then she'd get me the hell out of there, take me home, and stay with me as long as necessary.

Martha was just eighteen, and had graduated from high school just a few weeks earlier. She was supposed to start college in the fall, at Oberlin, out in Ohio. But she said she was going to spend the rest of the summer with me, taking care of me. That was hard work, let me tell you. A nurse came in once a day for a couple of hours, and took care of bathing me and things like that. But Martha did everything else. Emptying bed pans, getting me out of bed and into my wheelchair, doing my hair, and cooking wonderful meals straight out of *Bon Appétit*. And dealing with the speech therapist and the physical therapist and the nurse. She had a few friends in town, from the summers she'd spent there with me in the past, but she wouldn't hear of going out and having fun with them. They had to come over to my house, so she didn't see all that much of them. But she didn't complain one bit about anything or ever give a sign that she was tired or impatient. Well, that's not quite right. She would get a little impatient if she thought I wasn't trying hard enough in therapy. But she didn't get cross, just goaded me with some of her wonderful humor. "Mike [he was the physical therapist] tells me that you were being lazy today. I won't have it, Grammy. If you don't shape up, I'll have to ground you." Such impertinence! She always could make me laugh.

In August, Martha told me she'd postponed going to Oberlin. She could begin in January, or even the next fall, depending on how I was doing. Well, I was very upset by that. But there was no arguing with her, and my daughter and son-in-law were no use at all. But then, they never have been. I spoiled my daughter rotten, but I discovered something about people when Martha came along. You can only spoil children if they collaborate with you. Martha wouldn't do that. It didn't matter how many presents you gave her, she just wouldn't spoil.

Of course I felt terribly guilty about Martha staying with me. Don't tell me that guilt doesn't do you any good. If it's something you can't do anything about, it's a waste of time, of course, but in this case it really got me going. I started trying a lot harder with my therapy. As the months went by, my speech became almost normal again. I stall once in a while, but it's just for a moment. And I got back up on my feet, first with a walker, then just a cane. I don't use that anymore, either. I'm not going to win any ballroom dancing contests, and I'm not going to be jogging either, but I get around fine.

Most of the credit, so far as I'm concerned, goes to Martha. She won't hear of that, of course. "Grammy, there's no way to keep an old battleaxe like you down for long," she said. "I just lent a little moral support."

She's going to college now. But she transferred to Columbia, so she gets out here for a visit just about every other weekend. We were good friends before my stroke, but we're even closer now. She brings her friends out with her sometimes. Nice young people, they are, full of good humor, and smart as whips. But none of them is as special as Martha. I can tell they admire her, too. Sometimes I catch them watching when Martha and I are making each other laugh, and you can see that they envy what Martha and I have between us. One of them, a boy named Michael, told me last time he was out, "I really like coming here. No generation gap, if you know what I mean." I thought that was a great compliment, to me and to Martha. Don't you agree?

—Lucille, 71

The Psychologist

When my daughter Ella became pregnant for the first time, I vowed that I would not be one of those grandmothers who bored everyone I met, friend or stranger, with tales of my grandson or granddaughter. Well, that kind of resolution is made to be broken, and from the minute Lisa was born I've been talking about her nonstop. She was joined by a younger brother three years later, and then a little sister two years after that, and I talk about Ned and Jill a lot too, but I think the first one always holds a special place in a grandmother's heart. Besides, Lisa is a truly remarkable child. She's one of those rare people who's always looking out for everyone else. That's unusual enough in grown-ups, but it's an especially rare quality to find in a child.

Last year Lisa turned fourteen, and she decided that it was time for me to stop smoking. I've been going at it for decades, two packs a day. My late husband was worse than I am, but it wasn't cigarettes that killed him. He died in a construction accident. A crane collapsed and took down the scaffolding he was working on. I had been trying to stop smoking at the time—that was four years ago—but his death got me to smoking more than ever. Now, I've always been perfectly well aware that smoking was bad for me. These people who sue tobacco companies saying, "I had no idea," are a joke in my estimation. I'll also say that I've enjoyed every cigarette I've ever smoked. Vices are often pleasurable—that's what keeps people doing what they shouldn't.

At first I wasn't even aware that Lisa was determined to get me to stop smoking. She didn't take the blunt approach some people do. She didn't say to me, "Grandma, you're taking years off your life," for instance. I have a good friend who answers that kind of remark by saying, "Good!" She had a father who was in a nursing home for five years, and her mother hasn't been sure what year it is for the past ten, so my friend doesn't think much of old age. But then, she never married, and she doesn't have grandchildren to make her feel that there are some wonderful reasons to live as long as possible.

Anyway, Lisa didn't confront me like that, or say, "Grandma, your house smells like an ashtray." She just left a paperback book on how to stop smoking in the pile of mysteries I'm always reading. I thought my daughter had done that, and it wasn't until later that I discovered who the culprit was. Then I found a pamphlet about the "patch" mysteriously tucked into the television guide. I read the book and the pamphlet, and since I had a regular doctor's appointment coming up, I asked him for a prescription for one of the brands of patches they have on the market. He practically fell off his chair, since he's been trying to get me to stop for years. He was happy to give me the prescription, but he warned me that the patch didn't perform miracles all by itself—you still had to really want to stop.

Well, I guess I didn't want it enough, because it didn't work for me, although I know other people who've been successful with it. So there I was two months later, still puffing away. Then one day Lisa went with me to the supermarket. I just bought a few things, which came to ten dollars and twelve cents. I never have the right change—I keep putting it in a box and forgetting to take it out again. So I asked Lisa if she had the twelve cents. She rooted around in her backpack to find it, and out fell a park of cigarettes. I went into a state of shock. The thought of my beautiful granddaughter with a cigarette dangling out of her mouth made me ill. I held my tongue until we got to the car, and then I asked her how long she'd been smoking. I asked if her parents knew, and said that she ought to know better, seeing how hard it was for me to stop.

When I'd finished this little lecture, Lisa looked at me with her blue eyes and said, "You were fourteen when you started,

146

Grandma. I know because Mom told me. Most of my friends smoke. We enjoy it, and I only smoke about four a day. And, no, Mom and Dad don't know. How about that being our secret?"

I didn't know what to say. But Lisa had one more comment to make. "I don't know why parents and grandparents keep saying we kids shouldn't do what they did. It's kind of stupid. I mean, you married Grandpa when you were only seventeen. That's just three years away for me, but I suppose you'll tell me I'm too young when the time comes."

That did it. I said, "Lisa, I'll make a bargain with you. I'll stop smoking if you will. This time I'll really stop, I mean it."

Lisa said, "Okay. Okay, that's a deal. But if you go back to smoking, I do, too. Deal?"

"Deal," I said. And I did it. It wasn't easy, either, and it's probably just as well I live alone these days, because I find myself snapping at inanimate objects sometimes. But it's getting easier. I've been off cigarettes for six months. My daughter is very pleased with me. She was congratulating me on my six months without a cigarette a couple of weeks ago, and without thinking I let slip that I couldn't have done it without Lisa, who'd stopped too. Then I realized what I'd done and said, "Oh, dear, that was supposed to be a secret."

Ella started laughing. I asked her what was so funny. She said, "Well, since you've spilled your secret, I'll tell you one, but this conversation has to be off the record for both of us so far as Lisa is concerned."

I certainly didn't want Lisa to know I'd let the cat out of the bag, so I agreed.

Ella said, "Well, Mom, Lisa never did smoke. She carried that pack around in her backpack for ten days waiting for a chance to drop it on the floor."

"So it was all a plot?" I wasn't really surprised, somehow. I'd never quite come around to admitting it to myself, but in a way I kind of knew it.

Ella nodded. "Worked, didn't it?"

"Yes, it did, and for once in my life I'm happy to have been tricked. I hope this means Lisa's not planning to get married at seventeen, either."

My daughter laughed again. "I thought that was laying it on a little thick, to tell you the truth. That's the furthest thing from Lisa's mind. She's planning to go to college and become a psycholgist."

"Really?" I said. "I don't see why she has to bother with college, though. It seems to me that my granddaughter already is a psychologist."

—*Estelle, 55*

"Over the Rainbow"

When I was a little girl, just eight years old, my mother took me to see a movie that remains my favorite of all time to this very day. It was 1939 and the movie was *The Wizard of Oz*. I'd read the book, the first of the Oz books by

Frank L. Baum, the previous year, and I was in the middle of *Ozma of Oz* when the movie came out. Now, of course, 1939 is regarded as the greatest year in the history of Hollywood. Some of the other movies that year were *Gone With the Wind, Wuthering Heights, Ninotchka, Dark Victory, Gunga Din*, and *Goodbye, Mr. Chips*. There were half a dozen other classics, but I was too young to see any of those at the time, although I caught up with them in later years. Still, as much as I love *Gone With the Wind* and several of the others, none could ever quite supplant *The Wizard of Oz* in my affections.

I saw *The Wizard of Oz* in one of the old movie palaces in Boston, which added to the magic. I grew up in a town about twenty miles from Boston, and I'd been to a number of children's matinees at the small theater there, but it was my first visit to a big city movie theater. All that marble and gilt, and the grand staircases—it was like some kind of heaven. But it was the movie itself that transported me, right along with Dorothy, over the rainbow. Color movies were just coming in then, of course, and when Dorothy's farmhouse came to rest after being carried aloft by the tornado, and she opened the door, and the world outside was in color, I remember my heart jumping, and saying, "Oh, Mommy!" I don't think kids today can really understand how magical that seemed at the time. It was just breathtaking.

Of course, I identified completely with Judy Garland as Dorothy met the Scarecrow and the Tin Man and the Cowardly Lion on the yellow brick road. From that moment, I was a fan of Judy's for life. I saw all her movies after that. I remember my mother was a little worried about my seeing *Presenting Lily Mars* in 1943, which was Judy's first "adult" role—I was still only eleven—but of course it was utterly innocent by today's standards. I got every record Judy made over the years, and followed her trials and tribulations in the movie magazines. I was grown up, of course, by the time she started having her worst problems, and I sympathized with her deeply. In 1955, when Grace Kelly got the Best Actress Oscar for *The Country Girl* instead of Judy for her comeback in *A Star Is Born*, I was absolutely spitting mad. It wasn't that I didn't like Grace Kelly, I did, but that Oscar was Judy's by right. I still think so.

One year in the early 1960s when Judy was on television opposite *Bonanza*, my husband Jack and I got into one of our rare arguments over which one to watch, and he came home from work the next day with a second television set. Jack is a native Texan, and we were living in Austin then. He had to have his *Bonanza* and I had to have my Judy. I'd never seen Judy perform live, though of course I had her famous Carnegie Hall double album. In 1966, she appeared at the Houston Astrodome, with the Supremes as her opening act, and Jack surprised me with an anniversary present of tickets to the concert. We even spent the night in Houston. Judy was having her problems then, but she was in great form that night. I was in tears by the end of the evening. Tears of joy, of course.

I cried again, with great sadness, when she died in 1969. But of course I had all her records, and eventually, when VCRs came in, I managed to record most of her movies. I watch some of my favorites every year. I think I must know *Easter Parade* and *Summer Stock* by heart. Of course, I brought our daughter Lois up on Judy Garland, and when she had children, I tried to make them into fans. My grandson Johnny liked *The Wizard of Oz* when he was small, but that was about it with him. He's eighteen now, and I suppose when he gets to be my age he'll be nostalgic about Celine Dion, who does have a beautiful voice. My granddaughter Laurie, who's fourteen now, liked some of the others, but a lot of them she thought were pretty corny. And of course they are. Things do change.

These days Laurie is gaga about Ricky Martin, and I must say he's awfully good looking. But my love for Judy Garland did make an impression on her, and she proved it last year. We had a fire at our house, caused by some old wiring in the basement den. Fortunately, Jack had installed smoke alarms and put several fire extinguishers around the house. He was able to get the fire tamped down, the fire department arrived very fast, and only part of the den was really badly damaged. But it happened to be in a corner where our old LP records are stored. My Judy Garland albums were all destroyed. It was just awful. Of course, you can get a lot of them on CD. But there are some that are irreplaceable. Well, I was very upset, as you can imagine—look how I've been going on about Judy.

Last Christmas, about four months after the fire, my daughter Lois, her husband Guy, and the kids drove up to San Antonio, where Jack and I live now, from their home in Corpus Christi for a turkey dinner, as they always do. They were laden with presents—we do Christmas up in a big way in our family. There was one very large box I was curious about, and I snuck a look at it. It was to me from my granddaughter Laurie. But when we started opening all the presents, there was something else from Laurie for me, a lovely silver pin fashioned from the handle of an antique spoon. So I kind of forgot about the big box. Then, after everything else had been opened, Laurie got up and went to the tree and picked up the big box and brought it over to me.

"This only cost four dollars, Grandma," she said. "But I think you might like it."

Jack moved over a little on the sofa so that Laurie could put the box down beside me, since it was too big to hold in my lap. I got it unwrapped, and inside it there was a lot of that foam popcorn and then a second wrapped package. It had the shape of an old-fashioned LP set, and my heart started to beat a little faster in anticipation. I got the paper off that and when I saw the title I had to stop and put my hands to my face for a moment and take a deep breath. The cover read, "The Longines Symphonette Society proudly presents The Immortal JUDY GARLAND— 'Over the Rainbow' and 49 other master-performances."

I let out a shriek of joy. This was a very special recording that was put out more than thirty years ago. You couldn't even buy it in stores. I guess you had to be a member of the society, which was like a book club, and I'd never even owned it. It was one of the few albums I'd never been able to get my hands on. I picked up the album box and turned it over. The back cover was gold, and then you pulled out a second box in bright red with gold lettering. That had a heavy flap you folded back that listed the music on each of the five records it contained. Five records and fifty songs. One favorite after another. I could hardly believe my eyes. And what's more, the records were in perfect condition, not a scratch on them. Somebody had taken very good care of these for a very long time. Well, of course I started crying, the way I did at the Astrodome way back in 1966. And then Lois started crying and so did Laurie, and Jack and Guy and Johnny kind of looked at us the way men do in such situations.

When we women had pulled ourselves together, Laurie explained that she'd gone to a sale at the public library where people donate old books and the proceeds go to the library's purchasing fund. She said that she didn't usually even look at the table of old records—she has nothing but CDs, of course—but she just had a hunch. This was only a week after our fire, and she wondered if there might be an old Judy Garland record in the boxes on the table. And there was this huge special edition of Judy's songs. "I was going to buy it no matter how much it cost," Laurie said, "even if I had to grab the money out of my friend's hands. But it was only four dollars! I just grabbed it and hugged it."

Well, I practically leapt up from that sofa—no easy task at my age—and grabbed my granddaughter and hugged *her*. I've received a great many very nice presents over the years, but there aren't many that have meant more to me.

—*Lorna, 68*

Grandma for Mayor

ℛunning for mayor of our fair city was not my idea, I assure you. We call it a city—it has a population of just over a hundred thousand—but people from big cities like Philadelphia, New York, or Baltimore tend to call it a town. Okay, so we don't have any major professional sports teams or a world-famous museum. We have fine restaurants, good enough to surprise people from out of town with their sophistication, but gourmets do not make special trips to eat in them. Actually, that's not quite true. We do have a diner that's been in the same family for sixty years, and it's been written up in several national magazines. Diner aficionados do quite often go out of their way to track it down. It's got breakfasts that would make the National Heart Association wince, a classic meatloaf, and the best apple pie I've ever tasted anywhere.

We also get a lot of tourists, actually, since we're in the heart of Amish country. And there's a famous outlet mall out on the highway. The city itself boasts a large number of late-eighteenth-century houses, and there's an enclosed farmer's market that's one of the oldest in the country. There's a lot of theater going on, quite a number of art galleries, and we've had many top entertainers perform at the amphitheater in the very beautiful county park on the edge of town. In other words, we are not just a bump in the road.

This county is quite conservative, however, and our representative to Congress has been a Republican for the past fifty years. The city itself occasionally elects a Democratic mayor, but not nearly as often as a Republican. The Democrats always try to put up a good fight, however, and sometimes they prevail. That means about once every fifteen years. In 1995—our mayoral elections are always in odd-numbered years, which gives the Democrats at least a fighting chance, since fewer people go to the polls than in congressional and presidential years—the incumbent mayor was retiring. He was a Republican, but he was a good friend of mine and my husband's. I saw him constantly because I was the head bookkeeper for the city. Having a bookkeeper who is of the opposite party from the incumbent mayor is something of a tradition here. It makes people feel that there's less likely to be any financial hanky-panky.

The expected new Republican candidate was a man who owned a number of businesses in town. He was a terrific back-slapper to boot, and most people thought he was unbeatable. The two members of the City Council who were Democrats didn't want to throw away their careers by running against him, so the hunt was on for a sacrificial lamb to head the Democratic ticket. The Democratic committee decided my husband Jack, who's a lawyer, was the ideal man for the job. So they invited him for lunch and tried to persuade him that he was so respected around town that he might even pull off a surprise win. That was exactly the wrong argument. If they'd assured him he'd lose by a huge margin, he might have done it, but the last thing he wanted to be was mayor. But Jack had a suggestion for them. "What about Marcie?" he said. That's me.

Well, they were a bit taken aback by that idea. Jack was very funny imitating the looks on their faces for me over our pre-dinner scotch that evening. Their expressions passed from stunned to aghast to forced smiles in the course of about three seconds. I laughed, but also suggested that Jack might have consulted me before offering me up so casually as a sacrifice on the altar of democracy. He said, "Oh, come on, Marcie, you'd have great fun, and you know it."

So I considered all the fun I'd have, and the committee members considered whether or not I'd make them look foolish, and I came to the conclusion that it would be an interesting challenge, while the committee persuaded themselves that with my knowledge of city finances I'd be a respectable candidate. The fact that I was a deacon of the Episcopal Church was seen as a bonus. That might take some of the steam out of the usual Republican line that all Democrats were born sinners, and all Republicans exemplars of morality and family values. Forgive me, but I do like to tease just a bit.

Before making a final decision though, I thought it would be a good idea to consult our daughter Jenny, her husband Mark, and our two grandchildren: Susan, who was fourteen, and Mathew, who was eleven. Mark, whom I've always cherished, said, "Go get 'em." Jenny said that it might be nice to have me lecture the whole city instead of just her for a change. My daughter has a sense of humor. Susan and Mathew thought the idea was really "cool." Well, I liked to think of myself as cool back in the 1960s, when that word came in, and I kept using it even when it went out of fashion for about twenty years, and was glad that it had come back into favor and that my grandchildren would associate the word with me. I did warn Susan and Mathew, however, that they would probably get some flak from their friends. They said they could take it, so it was decided: Grandma for Mayor!

I won't bore you with any campaign speeches here. Suffice it to say that the campaign went quite well. I'm quite a good speaker. I'm empowered by the Episcopal Church to preside at weddings and funerals, although I can't conduct communion services, and I've had a good deal of experience over the years with public speaking. That wasn't a worry. And with my fiscal background, I did have some sensible enough ideas about city government. The polls gradually began to suggest that the election had become a genuine horse race. I don't trust polls for a minute, but at least people weren't running in the opposite direction at full speed while holding their noses.

And I did have fun. The best part of it was the efforts of my grandchildren. They were my most dedicated volunteers, stuffing envelopes, putting up posters, and decorating my campaign headquarters with bunting worthy of a presidential aspirant. We had a great time, and whenever I inched up another point or two in the polls they made me feel as though I was achieving some kind of immortality. Jack and I had always done a lot of things with Susan and Mathew, but there was something quite special about this particular adventure. At the end of one very long Saturday, Susan said to me, "You know, Grandma, I'm going to remember all this forever." That kind of got to me, I must admit.

The day before the election, I was racing all over town. I stopped by my campaign headquarters late in the afternoon to see how everyone was doing, and was alarmed to see Mathew with a very black eye and a bandage on his hand. "Mathew," I said, "are you okay? What happened to you?"

"I got into a fight with that stupid Tim Barber," he said.

I had a sinking feeling. "I hope it wasn't about me?"

"It sure was, Grandma," Mathew said, with considerable pride.

"I thought we'd agreed that you wouldn't take nasty cracks about me seriously, Mathew," I said.

"I know," Mathew said, "but I couldn't help it. He kept yelling, 'Your Grandma's a (expletive deleted) liberal.' "

"Well," I said, trying to ignore the expletive deleted, "I think I am pretty liberal, at least by the standards of this town."

"I know," Mathew said. "But to him "liberal" is a *really* dirty word. Worse than the other one. He uses the other one all the time."

I knew this was not the time to laugh, but it was very hard to keep a straight face. "In that case," I said, once I'd got hold of myself, "thank you for defending me."

"Anytime, Grandma," Mathew said, and gave me a big hug.

It's very nice for a woman to have a knight in shining armor, especially when he's eleven and your grandson.

On that last day, the final poll showed me winning. I knew better, but kept my mouth shut, so as not to discourage the troops. On election day itself, the ballots told a different story. Grandma was not, after all, going to be the next mayor of our fair city. I didn't lose badly, and the city newspaper, which had not endorsed me, complimented me on a well-run and dignified campaign. That's the mint sauce that goes so well with sacrificial lamb.

I was glad I had run. I'd made some important points that people might remember down the line when my opponent did something stupid. Of course, if I had been elected, I would have done something stupid, too, although it would no doubt have been a different kind of stupid. Politics aside—very much aside—I'm glad I ran for mayor because it brought me closer than ever to my grandchildren. And I like to hope that Susan was right, that it was an adventure she and Mathew will remember forever.

—*Marcie, 64*

7

unexpected pleasures

All human beings must deal with the fact that life is a matter of expecting the unexpected. That is as true for a grandparent as it is for a nine-year-old child. The unexpected event may be a setback, even a tragedy, but life must go on. Fortunately, the unexpected can also be something that brings us joy. An unexpected pleasure may come long after we have accepted the idea that something we have hoped for is not going to happen. A sudden wonderful moment, even quite a small one, can light up our lives even when things seem very dark. Laughter and relief can erupt just when we have steeled ourselves for disappointment.

The stories told by grandparents in this final

chapter are about unexpected pleasures. They are about the ways in which a grandchild can change everything for the better in an instant. You will meet grandparents who had become inured to the idea that that was something they would never be. The ever-fraught question of what name will be given to a grandchild is recounted with fond amusement. A grandson, wise and loving beyond his tender years, brings unexpected pleasure to what had promised to be a very gloomy Christmas Day. Another young grandson finds a way to restore the goodwill between his mother and her mother, leading the grandmother to give thanks for the existence of Rosemary Clooney.

Several of the stories in this chapter are about moving on, as new circumstance or new vistas open in the lives of families. In the final story a grandfather tells of a grandson who gets on his bicycle and makes an almost magical appearance where he is not expected to be. His small, almost prankish act of love is an affirmation of the special bond that exists between grandparents and children everywhere.

Better Late Than Never

Fritz and I thought we weren't going to be grandparents. Our daughter, Elise, was having far too successful a career to give much thought to children. She was an extremely bright girl from the start, always at the top of her class, and she even skipped the fourth grade entirely. She wasn't a wallflower, either, with

161

all brains and no social life. She had a steady boyfriend all through high school who was equally bright, and when they went off to the same college, we fully expected them to get married by the time they graduated. But that didn't happen. They're still friends, but Rob married another girl, and Elise got her eye firmly fixed on a corporate career. She went to Harvard Business School for her MBA and got a job with a Fortune 500 company with no problems—she had several wonderful offers.

There were men in her life, we met several of them over the years, but it wasn't until she was thirty-two that she got married. Her husband Will was a Wall Street lawyer, and they lived a very busy life. Elise moved up fast in her company and was the vice president in charge of an entire division by the time she was thirty-four. They didn't seem to have time for children, and we got the feeling neither Elise nor Will wanted them, either.

Fritz and I kept our mouths shut. None of that "When are you two going to have a baby?" stuff from us. We knew better. Of course we would have liked to be grandparents, but we recognized early on that Elise was a daughter who was going to make her own decisions. Most of our friends were grandparents, and sometimes things would get a little difficult. One couple couldn't stop talking about their grandchildren, and were always suggesting that Elise would "come around" to the idea of children eventually. We found that kind of annoying. Another couple, with whom we've always been very close, went out of their way *not* to talk about their grandchildren, which was almost worse. And my sister, who had four children and eventually nine grand-children, was absolutely impossible. Fortu-nately, she lives in California and we live in Delaware, so we didn't have to listen to her comments about Elise being "selfish" all the time. But then, my sister raises horses—she's got breeding on the brain.

We'd become resigned to the situation, when Elise told me she was trying to get pregnant. She was thirty-six then, and I guess it was one of those things you read about in the magazines where women suddenly realize that the biological clock is ticking. It had also become clear to her that she wasn't going to get to be the CEO of her company. The "glass ceiling" business. She had a chance to go to another company where there seemed to be a better chance of rising higher, but she thought that company was in more trouble than it was admitting, and turned the job down. She was right about that. The company ran into some rough waters, and was taken over by a bigger fish.

But after two years of trying, Elise still wasn't pregnant. Both she and Will went through all kinds of tests, and there shouldn't have been a problem, but there was. That's common enough, I guess, when women wait that late to have a first child. So Fritz and I thought that was that. Then, a year later—Elise was thirty-nine by then—we went up to New York for a visit. They usually took us out to

163

a top restaurant our first night in town, but Elise said we were going to have a quiet evening at their apartment for a change. It's an absolutely beautiful apartment on Park Avenue, and we were more than happy to spend an evening there. Elise is a very fine cook, and so is Will, which I think is a little unusual for people with such high-pressure careers. We had duck that night, and in the middle of the meal Will said, "Could you pass me some more of the sauce for the duck, Grandpa?"

Fritz reached for the sauceboat and then stopped and sat back in his chair. My fork was suspended halfway between the plate and my mouth. "Would you mind repeating that sentence, Will?" Fritz said. So Will did just that, word for word, and broke into a big grin. "That's what I thought I heard," Fritz said, matter-of-factly, and passed the sauce. "When's the baby due?"

I was still in shock. "Babies," Will corrected. "Twins." Elise was giggling in a way I hadn't heard since she was about fourteen. Well, then of course we all leapt up from the table and embraced one another, everyone talking at once. It turned out that Elise had been taking fertility pills. I'm glad she hadn't told me. I would have worried that she'd end up in the newpapers with quintuplets or something.

And so three years ago Fritz and I finally became grandparents. After all those years of telling ourselves that it wasn't important, we've turned into the most doting grandparents imaginable. We're under strict orders to cut back on the presents. Little Jimmy and Janey have become the light of our lives—and made our social life much easier in terms of dealing with our other friends who are grandparents. I didn't even mind it when the couple who were always saying that Elise would "come around" were able to say, "I told you so." On the other hand, my sister seems quite annoyed by the whole thing. I can tell her grandparent stories tit for tat, and she never liked competition. What's more, none of her grandkids are twins. You can top anything with a twin story, I've found.

—*Grace, 71*

And Then Came March?

$\mathcal{M}$y husband's name is Brian, and we named our son Brian Jr. So of course when Brian got married, my husband was looking forward to having a Brian III in the family. Personally, I think that kind of thing can get carried too far. There's no sense pretending that you belong to a long line of kings or popes. And we're quite ordinary middle-class people. I mean it's one thing if the family is distinguished. Like Adlai Stevenson III, who was the first man I ever voted for to be president, back in 1956 when I'd just turned twenty-one. After all, his great-grandfather was vice president of the United States, so there was good reason to continue the name. But my husband said this was a democracy, and ordinary people had just as much right to make a big thing out of a name as rich, important people did. You can't really argue with that, and I try never to argue with Brian anyway.

But there were a few roadblocks in the way of having a Brian III in the family. Our son married a girl named June. She's pretty as can be, and very bright, but she has what I would call a whimsical streak. For example, there's the welcome mat at the front door of Brian and June's house. Our last name is Standish. So June had a mat made that reads: "Don't be Off-Standish. Ring the Bell." Now, there are people who seem to think this is cute, but Brian and I think it's a bit much. Not that we ever said anything. I think the expression on my husband's face the first time we saw it was enough to tell the story. But he just said, "Quite a mat," and June gave him one of her big smiles.

So we weren't too surprised that when June and Brian Jr. had their first child she was named April. Yes, it was a girl, and my husband was so disappointed it wasn't a boy, he hardly cared what she was called. Of course, he fell in love with his granddaughter in about two weeks flat. She was very pretty and bubbly, just like her mother, but with my brown eyes. Everyone notices that.

Two years later there was another little girl. And she was called May. We've always marveled at the way our son can introduce his family with a straight face. "This is my wife June, and my daughters April and May." He says it just as though they were named Sally,

Barbara, and Jenny. My husband gets around the whole thing, if the whole family is together, by saying, "This is my daughter-in-law June, my son Brian Jr., and my granddaughters May and April." He thinks by breaking up that April, May, June sequence nobody will notice. Actually some people don't.

Well, there we were with two granddaughters, absolute charmers both of them, but no Brian III. And for a while it looked as though we wouldn't get one. Five years went by after May was born, and then suddenly June was pregnant again. I told my husband, "Now, don't be disappointed if it's another girl. That's very likely, you know." Brian looked at me and said, "Well, I don't care what it is so long as it isn't named after a month. You can't very well call a kid September." That was the month the baby was due. "No," I said, "but you could probably get away with August, especially if it was a boy. That *is* used as a boy's name sometimes." Brian said, "God help us!"

The baby came right on schedule. June never has any problems with that. I remember being in labor with Brian Jr. for nine hours, but June always gets it done in an hour flat. I envy her that.

The phone call came that it was a boy. Brian Jr. was all excited when he called and of course my husband was beside himself. Now his name could be carried on into a third generation. But I warned him against assuming that. "Don't count on it," I said. "You're dealing with June here."

We didn't go to the hospital. June was going

home the next day. June's so healthy, I think she could probably have gotten up and walked out an hour later. So we went over to see her and the new baby boy the next afternoon. June was sitting in the living room in the big easy chair, holding the baby. He had a very healthy look to him. Strong. And of course, the first words out of my husband's mouth, even though I'd told him to wait a bit, were, "What are you calling him?"

June looked straight up at my husband and beamed at him. She had this look in her eye that worried me. "March," she said.

I put my hand on Brian's arm, hoping to calm him down. But all he said was, "Better than August." I thought, what's gotted into the man? I'd expected an explosion. I thought maybe he was so glad it was a boy he just didn't care about the name.

June looked surprised, too. And the baby suddenly started to howl. That set June laughing. Then she stopped and patted the baby and said, "It's all right, little Brian. It's all right. I was just kidding." And she looked up at my husband again and said, "His name, of course, is Brian Standish III."

I looked over at my husband, and the tears were rolling down his cheeks. I hadn't seen him cry since I don't know when. His voice was kind of choked, but he managed to get out, "Thank you, June. I always knew you were a great girl."

And so now we have three generations of Brians.

—Ginny, 63

$\mathcal{M}$y daughter Nancy and her husband Bud are terrific parents to my two granddaughters Emily and Carla. Church, PTA meetings, family vacations—they do everything parents are supposed to do. And the girls are very polite and neat. But they're six and five and they have their own way of dealing with the world, and sometimes it seems as though they're really from another planet. Maybe it's because they're so close in age; maybe it's because they're quite exceptionally bright; and maybe it's just television and the way things are now. But sometimes they do things that are really off-the-wall.

Take their little visit to see Nancy's friend Norine last Christmas. Now, I have to be honest about this, but I've never really liked Norine. She and Nancy had been friends since they were children. Or at least Nancy has regarded them as friends. I've always thought that Nancy was really just an audience for Norine, someone to impress. Norine is from a very rich family, and she's always thought she had better taste than anyone on the planet. She's the kind of woman who makes a great point of looking down on Martha Stewart. I think Martha Stewart can be a bit much at times, but she's so clever and upbeat that she gets away with it. But from Norine's point of view, Martha Stewart isn't too much, she's not classy enough. Too commercial, not restrained enough to be taken seriously. And Nancy has always been sort of goggle-eyed about Norine's "taste." I've always found it annoying. So I just loved the stunt my granddaughters pulled.

This happened the Saturday before Christmas. Norine and her husband live in what can only be called a mansion, one of the grandest houses in town. They have no children and rattle around in this showplace all by themselves. Of course, they're always entertaining, but they seldom have houseguests, even though they have seven bedrooms—all of them decorated to the nines.

Norine's Christmas tree is always something to behold. I'm hardly in her set, but I have seen it a few times because I do volunteer work at the major hospital and Norine's husband is on the hospital board, so Norine has a tea party for the volunteers every couple of years. She collects Christmas ornaments by Radko, you know, *Christopher* Radko, who produces different ornaments every year and gets written up in all the design magazines. Some of them are wonderful, but others are extremely peculiar, from my point of view, and sometimes just plain ugly. But they cost about forty dollars apiece, and Norine must have 300 of them. Add that up!

So of course, Nancy and the girls were just gaga about the tree—it was the first time Emily and Carla had seen it. Then Norine suggested that they have some coffee and cookies in the kitchen, but the girls asked if they could just sit and look at the tree. Norine looked a little wary, but Nancy quickly said, "Now, you know you musn't touch any of the ornaments. Not even touch." And the girls quickly promised they wouldn't. So off go Norine and Nancy to the kitchen.

The tree itself was quite something, of course, but underneath it were about forty packages. They were wrapped in exquisite paper—Nancy assumed Norine must have bought it in Europe because she's never seen anything like it around here. And the presents were arranged under the tree in a way you only see in magazines. As though they were just to be looked at and never opened.

Well, Nancy and Norine had their espresso and cookies—from Harrod's in London, of course—and went back to the living room. And there were Emily and Carla happily sitting on the floor by the tree. They'd been very busy. You guessed it, they'd managed to unwrap about twenty of the packages. Being well brought up little girls, they'd carefully folded the paper after unwrapping each package, but this nicety was lost on Norine. Nancy screamed when she saw what her girls had done, but Norine was momentarily speechless. Then she muttered, "And the open house is tomorrow!" Well, Nancy said she'd buy new paper, no matter what it cost, and stay up all night if she had to, rewrapping everything.

By this time, Norine had regained her grip on life, and she turned to Nancy and said, "Get out of my house, and take those miserable little demons with you." Nancy grabbed the girls and headed for the door, jabbering her apologies. But Norine yelled, "Don't even try to apologize. Just get out and stay out!"

On the way home, Emily and Carla quite correctly pointed out that they'd only been told not to touch the ornaments. Nobody had said anything about the packages. Nancy told me on the phone she had thought she was going to drive off the road when they said that. She called me as soon as she got home, of course, to tell me the story. I'm afraid it was all I could do to keep from laughing. I thought I was going to have to stuff a handkerchief in my mouth. And then at the end of the story, Nancy wailed, "And she hadn't even invited us to the open house." And at that I let go and started laughing. I thought I was going to choke, I was laughing so hard. I know, it's just terrible of me. And Nancy said, "*Mother,* when the girls do things like this I know just who they got it from. It's you!" And then she hung up.

It's supposed to be awful to have your daughter hang up on you, but I'm afraid I was still laughing. And, you know, I think Nancy was probably right about the girls getting it from me. My mother used to say when I was a girl that I must be a changeling, like in all the fairy tales. That was back before space aliens became the popular excuse. I told Nancy that, when she called back a half hour later to apologize. And not only did she forgive me, but the whole business finally cured her of her attachment to Norine. About time, I'd say. I'm very gateful to my demon granddaughters for that.

—*Lorna, 63*

The Stockings Hang by the Fire

𝒯wo years ago, at the end of August, my daughter was killed in an automobile accident. Her car was rammed by a drunk in a pickup truck. He's in prison now, but that does nothing to bring back my beloved Ellen, or to make life easier for her husband Milt, or for my grandsons Eddy and Bobby. How we all got through those first few months I don't know, but somehow we did. Things were still very low in December, and it was obviously going to be a sad Christmas. But it was Christmas nevertheless, and for the sake of Eddy and Bobby, we had to try to make the best of it.

Milt came over to my house one evening while the boys were at a neighbor's house— his neighbors were just wonderful about helping out, something you can't always count on these days. Poor Milt was really distraught about Christmas. That was something Ellen had always been in charge of. We make a lot of Christmas in my family, and Ellen took enormous pleasure in decorating the house for her husband and sons, and buying presents and making them look like a million dollars even if they didn't cost that much. Milt just didn't know if he could handle it by himself, because every time he thought about it he became so emotional. He asked me if I could help him, and of course I said I would.

Milt paid for everything, but I did almost all the shopping for presents, and the wrapping, and I went over to decorate the house for him. I got out all the usual treasures, which was difficult for me to deal with, too, but it seemed important to give Eddy and Bobby a sense of continuity. Milt did put the tree up, and Eddy and Bobby and I decorated it together. Eddy was nine at the time and Bobby was seven, so they did the lower branches while I teetered around on a stepladder and did the top. It looked very festive by the time we were through, although not as beautiful as it had when Ellen did it—but I tried to put that thought out of my mind.

I went over early Christmas morning to get the turkey in the oven, and then we had a big breakfast before opening any presents. That was a rule when Ellen was little, and she'd carried on the tradition with her own family. As usual we had eggs and sausages and blueberry muffins. We wouldn't have Christmas dinner until about three in the afternoon, so we needed sustenance. While the muffins were baking, I went into the living room to make sure everything was alright. I'd put the boys' stockings in a drawer for Milt to fill after the boys went to bed. Ellen had always put in oranges and apples and unshelled nuts, with candies underneath them and a special little wrapped treat in the bottom. I was glad to see that Milt had remembered to put them up on the fire screen.

But then Milt came in and when he saw the stockings, he said, "Oh, I'm glad you took care of the stockings. I was so upset last night I'd completely forgotten about them."

I looked at him in astonishment. "I didn't

do it," I said. But there they were. I'd made the stockings for the boys myself, of red-and-white felt with their names embroidered at the top. Milt and I looked at each other, and wondered who had been playing Santa Claus. We decided it must have been Eddy, which turned out to be right. He'd tiptoed in to look at things very early that morning, and when he saw there were no stockings, he'd taken matters into his own hands, finding the candies in a kitchen cabinet and taking the fruit out of the refrigerator. I'd already tucked the little wrapped treat in the toe of each one.

It was very cold that Christmas Day, and Milt had started a fire in the fireplace just before breakfast. It was burning away nicely when we came in to open the presents. The boys went at the stockings first, taking out one thing at a time—we always liked to stretch things out. Eddy was just beaming as he watched Bobby reach into his stocking and pull out the fruit. I was so proud of him for taking matters into his own hands and making sure the stocking was there for his little brother.

Then Bobby got to the bottom of his stocking, and let out a shriek. He pulled his hand out, and it was covered with brown goo. Because of the fire, the chocolates, which weren't wrapped, had melted. Well, Eddy and Milt and I all started laughing, and then Bobby realized what had happened, too, and started licking the chocolate off his hands. Of course it got all over his face, and we all laughed some more, including Bobby. We hadn't expected to have laughter in the house

175

that morning, and it was the most wonderful sound in the world.

I probably shouldn't say this, some people will think it's foolish, but as we all sat there laughing our heads off, I thought I heard another, softer laugh in the room. Ellen's laugh. I think Milt heard it, too.

—*Audrey, 62*

Thank You, Rosemary Clooney

I'm going to have to fill you in on a good deal of family history before I get around to explaining what Rosemary Clooney has to do with my life, so just bear with me.

This story goes back to the birth of my daughter, Lily-Anne. It was lucky that she turned out to be a girl. During my pregnancy, all I heard from my husband Fred were the words "she" and "her." "I hope she's as pretty as you are." "What are we going to name her?" It began to get on my nerves, to tell the truth. What was going to happen if by some ridiculous chance the baby turned out to be a boy? In fact, I would have liked it to be a boy, although I kept my mouth shut about that. You see, I come from a family of five girls. I was the oldest, and every time my mother went off to the hospital I prayed that this time she'd come home with a brother for me. But it just wasn't meant to be.

Anyway, Fred got his wish, on April 20, 1970. Lily-Anne came screaming into the world after a mere five hours of labor. Fred was beside himself, running up and down the hospital corridors passing out pink cigars made of bubble gum. Lord knows where he got hold of those. We were a family now. The baby was healthy, I was exhausted but healthy, and Fred was behaving like a lunatic with his bubble gum cigars. The name Lily-Anne joined both sides of the family. My mother was Lily and Fred's mother was Anne.

As the years went by, Fred brought a whole new meaning to the phrase "Daddy's little girl." So far as he was concerned, our daughter could do no wrong. If Fred ever said "no" to Lily-Anne, I wasn't around to hear it. Discipline was left strictly up to me, although I will say Fred didn't try to stop me from doing my job in that department. Someone had to, and it wasn't going to be Fred. I take full credit for the fact that Lily-Anne didn't turn out to be spoiled rotten.

There was even a period when I became jealous of my own daughter, which may sound strange to some people, but I know other women who have gone through the same thing. Before Lily-Anne was born, Fred would come through the front door in the evening calling, "Where's my girl?" meaning me. But by the time Lily-Anne could walk, that had changed to "Where's my little angel?" I couldn't help thinking sometimes, "What about me? Whatever happened to me?" Finally, it got to me, and one day when he came home calling for Lily-Anne I happened to be coming into the hallway, and I burst into sobs and ran upstairs. I wasn't one to cry, and that incident shocked Fred into realizing what was happening. After that it was, "Where are my favorite girls?" Sometimes Fred didn't think, but he loved me and he wasn't dumb. My sobs got the message across.

Of course, Lily-Anne worshipped the ground her father walked on. So she was traumatized when he died years later after a long battle with cancer. He was first diagnosed when Lily-Anne was fourteen. The doctors thought they'd caught things in time, but they were wrong. He was back in the hospital in six months, and he died five months after that. Lily-Anne was very strong during this whole period, very helpful to me and extremely loving with her father. I think Fred lived several months longer than he might have just because of her. But the trouble was that she had convinced herself that he wouldn't—just couldn't—die. He was only forty-seven when he went. I had been prepared for it for months, but even so it was awfully hard to lose my beloved husband and best friend in life so young. But I had to put my own emotions aside, because Lily-Anne just went to pieces. The worst of it was that in some irrational way she blamed me for his death. She got it into her head that I hadn't cared enough, prayed hard enough, gotten him different doctors—whatever. The year following his death was the worst I've ever lived through.

Gradually, things got better between us, but in some ways they were never the same. Lily-Anne stopped blaming me, but although she never said it openly, I knew that in her heart of hearts she wished that it had been me rather than her father that had gotten cancer. When it came time to apply for college, all the ones Lily-Anne chose were out of state. I didn't say anything—that would only have made things worse. So she went off to North Carolina. We talked on the phone at least once a week and she came home for Christmas, but she got summer jobs that kept her away, too, so I didn't see her for more than a few weeks out of the year.

At the beginning of December, during her junior year, she called me and said, "I have a big surprise for you! Now, don't get mad at me, Mommy, because I'm very, very happy. Terry and I got married yesterday!" I wasn't mad, I was speechless. She'd mentioned a young man named Terry a couple of times, but quite casually. Now she said, "Terry's a dream. You're going to adore him, and we're going to come spend Christmas with you and then go to his parents in New York for New Year's. I love Terry very much. And I love you, Mommy. I'll call in a few days and we'll make Christmas plans, okay? 'Bye!"

As I said earlier, I'm not much of a crier, but I burst into tears with the phone still in my hand. It wasn't because Lily-Anne had gotten married so suddenly, or because there wouldn't be a formal wedding, or because I'd never even met the young man. It was because she'd said, "I love you, Mommy." She hadn't said those words to me since her father's death.

Lily-Anne was right. Terry was a dream. Handsome and intelligent and with a wonderful sense of humor. We got along splendidly from word one, and we had a wonderful Christmas that year.

It didn't take long for those two kids to start a family. In fact, it took seven months. I didn't let that bother me. I remembered what Nancy Reagan said about the birth of her daughter Patti, "Go ahead and count." Besides, I not only had a grandchild, but it was a boy. And he was called Frederick. I got to see little Freddie that summer. Lily-Anne and Terry came and spent two weeks with me. Then they went back to finish college. Terry came from quite a wealthy family, so there wasn't any trouble about money. They liked Lily-Anne as much as I liked Terry, and I got along well with them in our phone conversations. I didn't get to meet them for another year and a half, though, and that was when they came and stayed with me on a visit to see Lily-Anne, Terry, and Freddie. Because something quite surprising and quite wonderful had happened.

The best job offer Terry got after college was from a major national printing company right here where I live—the same company that my own Fred had been an executive at. So my daughter and her husband and my grandson were living just a ten-minute drive away. That seemed almost too good to be true, but it turned out to be wonderful for all of us. It made my life much richer, and they had a ready-made baby-sitter. Lily-Anne even gave me a very nice compliment. She said, "I hope you can do as much to keep Freddie in line as you did for me, Mommy."

Life was very pleasant. But now I have to introduce a new character in this story—and we will get to Rosemary Clooney, I promise. The new character is Roger. I met Roger when Fred was in the hospital during his last month. Roger's wife Susan was dying of cancer, too, and we kept running into each other. So we started having coffee in the hospital cafeteria, and commiserating with each other. We got along very well, although we were seeing each other through a fog of grief. Roger's wife died a week before Fred did, and I sent flowers to the funeral and Roger did the same for me. But then he moved away almost immediately. He sent me a little note, saying he was going to travel for a while, but would be in touch. But I didn't hear a word from him for ten years.

Then one day the doorbell rang and it was Roger. It took me a moment to realize who he was. He'd been in the Far East all that time, and had made some very good business investments. But he'd finally gotten homesick for America. He apologized for never writing, but said that at first he was just trying to lose himself in work, and then it had seemed presumptious to get back in touch. Now that he was back in town, however, he'd decided to look me up, since he'd asked around and found out that I'd never remarried. He hadn't either, although he said he'd come close once.

So Roger and I got to know each other all

over again, and much better than we had the first time around. My son-in-law Terry got along with him very well, and Lily-Anne was polite, but there was kind of a tension there. Roger and I had become very close, and although we were discreet and never spent the night together, Lily-Anne seemed to be somewhat unhappy with our relationship. I thought of pointing out that I'd never criticized her for being pregnant when she was married, but decided to keep my mouth shut. I'd never had more than dinner with a man since Fred died, and hardly thought I had anything to apologize for. Besides, I was only fifty-eight, and Roger only sixty. We were hardly over the hill.

After about ten months, Roger proposed to me and I accepted, but before we had a chance to tell Lily-Anne about it—in fact we were going to do it that very day—Lily-Anne and Freddie were over at my house on a Saturday afternoon, just stopping off to say hello. Now, Roger and Freddie, who was seven, had really hit it off. Roger is a wonderful storyteller, and Freddie loved to hear about all the exotic places Roger had been. That afternoon, while Lily-Anne and Freddie were sitting around the kitchen table drinking lemonade, Roger came in, and Freddie said, "Hi, Grandpa!"

Lily-Anne's expression changed instantly. Suddenly she had that clouded, sullen look I'd seen for so long after her father's death. And she actually screamed, "He's not your grandfather! That man is not your grandfather." And she stood up and grabbed Freddie's hand and rushed out of the house, with Freddie protesting loudly.

Roger and I looked at each other in shock. I'd told him about what I'd gone through with Lily-Anne the year after her father's death, but that things had worked out in the end. Roger is a very smart man, and he'd said, "I'm not so sure she's put that completely behind her." How right he had been!

Roger and I both agreed that it was best just to let things drift for a couple of days, but for different reasons. I wanted to give Lily-Anne time to calm down, while Roger wouldn't hear of me calling her first, even though he understood why I might want to. Two days went by, and then I got a call from Terry asking both me and Roger over for dinner. I asked Terry why the invitation wasn't coming from Lily-Anne, and he said not to worry, things were going to be all right. I told him that Roger and I were planning to marry, and he said, yes, Roger had called him at work to tell him that, and that he and Freddie had figured that out, too. That was why Freddie had called Roger Grandpa. I said, "But Lily-Anne hadn't figured it out?" And Terry sort of sighed and said, "Oh, of course, but she didn't want to deal with it. Things are different now, you'll see."

When we arrived for dinner, Roger and I were quite nervous, even so. Terry answered the door, and took us into the living room. We sat down and then Lily-Anne and Freddie came into the room. Lily-Anne said, "First of all, I want to apologize for my inexcusable outburst the other afternoon. The only thing I can say is that sometimes that past jumps up and grabs you, and you don't know who you are for a minute. The other thing I want to tell you is that your grandson has had his bags packed to come live with you for two days, and that he has something to say, too."

Freddie, who had been hanging back a little, said, "Well, it's just this thing I read a little while ago in a magazine. It was about a famous old singer who got married to a man she'd known a long time. Now get this! She said that they were getting married because of her grandkids, so they'd have somebody else to call Grandpa. The name of the singer was Rosemary Clooney. Do any of you guys remember her?"

Roger said, "I sure do. She's still terrific. I think I have an album of hers around someplace, if you want to hear it."

And I assured Freddie that I was a fan, too. In fact, of course, I'm more than a fan now. I simply worship Rosemary Clooney, with good reason. Because it turned out that Freddie had told his mother, my dear daughter Lily-Anne, all about the Rosemary Clooney story on the way home after she'd thrown her fit. It had taken a couple of days for Lily-Anne to come around, but it worked. So here's to my very smart grandson, and to Rosemary Clooney.

—*Sylvia, 59*

A Farewell Wave

My wife Alta-Mae and I had always planned on retiring to Florida eventually. Alta-Mae is from Georgia originally, and she never was all that happy about northern winters. As for me, the prospect of playing golf almost year 'round was a big draw. I had built up a very successful contracting business just outside Philadelphia, but I had figured long ago that if neither of our two sons, Rich and Jimmy, wanted to take the business over, then I'd simply sell it when the time came. As it happened, both boys decided to go into it with me after college. They are very smart young men, if I do say so, and they helped build the company beyond anything I'd ever anticipated. We worked out a deal that would give me and Alta-Mae a very nice retirement income, and I set my retirement for sixty-five.

The only unhappy part of moving to Florida was leaving our grandchildren behind. Rich has two daughters, Allie and Cindy, and Jimmy has a daughter, Mary, and a son, named Henry after me, but called Hank. It's awfully nice to watch your grandchildren grow up in the same town you've lived in all your life. It gives things a kind of continuity that isn't too common anymore. We had a wonderful time over the years with all four of the grandkids, but I always had a special feeling for Hank, I guess because he was the only boy. By the time of my retirement, Rich's girls were both in high school, and would be going off to college before too long anyway.

We'd already promised we'd be on hand for their high school graduations, though.

Mary, Jimmy's daughter, was Alta-Mae's favorite, although she tried not to show it. They had the same kind of bubbly sense of humor, and they were always giggling together about something. Mary was in eighth grade when we left for Florida. She'd insisted on teaching Alta-Mae how to use the Internet so they could E-mail each other as often as they wanted, which turned out to be just about daily.

It was hardest leaving Hank behind, at least for me, and in some ways for Alta-Mae, too. He was only ten, and I was very much aware of how many things we'd miss doing together during his teenage years. I'd been taking him to Phillies games since he was six, which was an education in cheering along the perpetual losers in life. Every now and then, though, we'd catch a game where they actually managed to beat a first-place team, Atlanta or Houston or whatever, and that was always a special thrill. When the time came to move to Florida, I made a pact with Hank. If the Phillies ever got into the playoffs, I'd come up and we'd go to a couple of the games. One thing about being a contractor is that you always know somebody who can get you tickets to something like that.

Still, I knew Hank was upset we were moving away. He didn't make a big thing of it, but I'd catch him with this faraway expression on his face that last spring before we moved, and I knew what he was thinking. The day the moving van came to load up all our earthly possessions, he came over and watched for a while. He was fascinated seeing how so much furniture got stacked into such a small space, but after a while it began to get to him a little. I took him off for an ice-cream cone, and we talked about how we'd go deep-sea fishing when he came down to Florida to visit.

The van wasn't due to reach our new home in Boca Raton for six days, and we were going to take a leisurely trip down, stopping off to see some of Alta-Mae's relatives in Georgia, among other things. And there was no need to get on the road the same day the van left, so we spent that night at Jimmy's house, and Rich and his family came over for a big barbecue. The next morning, which was a Saturday, we planned to get on the road about ten. We said our good-byes to Jimmy and his wife Lisa, and to Mary and Hank, and then drove over to Rich's house for a final hug there.

I guess I need to explain something about the roads out of town here. Rich's house was about a mile from Jimmy's, and a mile after that there's a fork in the road. The right-hand fork takes you around through some newer neighborhoods, and the left-hand fork leads to the highway that takes you to I-95, where we'd head south. There's a small rocky island in the middle of the fork, with a bit of grass and some spindly bushes but no trees. Well, we were driving along, with me at the wheel for the first leg of the journey, and as we approached the fork Alta-Mae, who has the eyesight of a hawk, said, "Will you look at that! Slow down, Henry, and give a honk."

And there on that rocky little island was Hank, leaning on his bicycle, peering at the passing cars. And then he saw us and began waving. He'd gotten on his bike and raced the two miles out there while we were saying our good-byes at Rich's house. Well, I slowed as much as I could get away with in the traffic, and Alta-Mae waved and I gave three honks of the horn, and he gave us this big smile as we passed by, waving like mad.

Now, I'm not a man who cries easily, but I have to admit that after we passed Hank I had to take off my glasses for a minute and wipe my eyes. I suppose part of it was sadness, but there was more to it than that. I was really touched that he'd bicycle all that way just to give us a last wave farewell. It was a really special moment in my life.

That was a year ago. Hank will be coming down for a two-week visit next month. I've got that deep-sea fishing expedition all lined up. And, not entirely by coincidence, the Phillies are going to be playing the Marlins during that period, so we're going to drive down to Miami to see a game. We figure the Phillies at least ought to be able to beat the Marlins. But of course you never know. It'll just be awfully nice to see Hank again.

—*Henry, 66*